GUIDE TO MANAGING PEOPLE

GUIDE TO MANAGING PEOPLE

How to Control People
Through the Secrets
of Dynamic Leadership
and Supervision

James K. Van Fleet

Author of: How to Use the
Dynamics of Motivation

Parker Publishing Company, Inc.   West Nyack, New York

What This Book Will Show You

R. Earl Allen, a prominent Baptist minister and author, once told me that a good sermon ought to do four things. "It should stretch the mind, tan the hide, warm the heart, and provoke the will!" he said.

I don't think this introduction to my book will accomplish all that, but if it's going to do the job I want it to do, it will at least give you some idea of the value of the pages that lie ahead; it will succinctly and summarily tell you in short order what you're getting into.

You see, I know that in today's hurried world, you and I don't have the time to read books as leisurely as we used to. Many times, a quick glance at the preface and the table of contents will tell you whether you want to read a particular book or not.

So I'll say right here and now that *this book is written about how to manage—how to supervise—how to influence other people.*

It Will Show You How You Can Control Other People!

And it will do that by revealing certain secrets to you about people and by giving you some practical down-to-earth, concrete examples of how other people did it.

And it'll do that in simple and precise easy-to-understand language. You'll find no high flown theories of applied psychology here. There are no frills or fluff. It's all meat.

A few years ago, when I was vacationing in Port Malabar, Florida, I visited the space center at Cape Kennedy which lies just a few miles north of the Port. There I met several of the NASA officials who run the center.

"What's the hardest job for you in the space program?" I asked Gordon Hammill, one of the directors there at the Cape.

"Controlling people," he said without a moment's hesitation. "Hydrogen and oxygen always behave exactly the same way all the time under certain set conditions. But when you add two or more people together along with a liberal sprinkling of the fair sex—well, no one can accurately predict what the outcome will be!

"But all joking aside," he went on, "supervision, executive management, control of people—all these are the most difficult areas for us here at Cape Kennedy. You can teach a man which button to punch on a machine, but I've yet to find the book that'll tell me which button to punch on him!

"We need more good books, more manuals, more publications on how to handle people—on how to control them. Leadership is a sadly neglected subject in our high schools and colleges today. We're turning out technicians by the hundreds and the thousands. But leaders? No!

v

"And it's harder to learn when you're out of school. Plain lack of time gets in your way. Even the government publications they give us to use for guidance in handling personnel problems are worse than the few textbooks there are on the subject. They're all full of governmental gobbledy-gook, and written by some GS 12 or 13 who doesn't know any more about the subject than I do; probably not as much.

"Seriously, we do need good readable books with practical examples that will show how Joe Smith and Sam Brown solved their problems of management—how they controlled their people."

How to control people. That was Gordon Hammill's problem—his question. I think this book is his answer—and perhaps yours, too!

CONTENTS

THE 6TH SECRET

THE 7TH SECRET

Use the Law of Reversal — and Get Results

Paul Meyer, the president of Success Motivation Institute of Waco, Texas, the country's leading producer of recorded courses in personal motivation, executive development, and sales training, learned early in his highly successful business career to *use the law of reversal to get results.*

Mr. Meyer found that if he offered a man self-respect and self-reliance in his job, he would in turn receive benefits from that man for himself by the simple (but little understood) *law of reversal.*

"If a man wants more opportunity to prove his worth, offer him the responsibility of a task requiring his initiative and his ingenuity and the complete freedom to use his own ideas to accomplish the mission you've assigned to him," says Mr. Meyer.

"At the same time, make sure he understands that he has the full responsibility for the success or failure of the job you've given him to do.

"The chances are good that the man will work like the very dickens to make the project succeed for you. And when he does make good, he'll have gained the *security of accomplishment* and the *recognition of others* for a job well done.

"The thing is, you've got to give a man the opportunity to satisfy most of his primary desires right on the job before he'll go all out for you," Mr. Meyer goes on to say. "But before you can do that, you must know what's important to each one of them.

"You must know what every employee of yours wants, and you must help him satisfy those wants. Don't expect anything in return from him unless you *do something for him first. You must put the law of reversal into motion yourself if you want to get results.*"

Mr. Meyer knew that if he would *offer a man security, gain, and recognition on his job,* that man would go all out to produce for him. And Mr. Meyer, my friend, was a millionaire when he was only 27! He started from scratch, too; no silver spoon!

Six concrete benefits you can get by using the law of reversal.

If you, too, will learn how to satisfy your employees' desires on the job, perhaps you'll become a millionaire just like Mr. Meyer. And if not, at least you'll still be able to profit by having employees who will—

    1. *Respect and have confidence in you.*

      2. *Give you their willing obedience, their loyal
        cooperation, and their wholehearted support.*

3. Work with initiative, ingenuity, and enthusiasm.
4. Work together as a team with high spirit, morale, and esprit, with purpose and direction toward a common goal.
5. Feel that they belong where they are.
6. Work as hard as they can to make a profit—for you!

Use the law of reversal to satisfy a man's primary desires.

Just exactly how do you go about gaining those six benefits? The same way Mr. Meyer did; by offering a man the chance to satisfy his primary desires while he's on the job.

For instance, did you know that off the job, most of us spend the bigger part of our take-home pay to buy those material things which will satisfy our *four primary desires?* And these four primary desires are—
1. *A feeling of security.*
2. *A feeling of pride or satisfaction of one's ego.*
3. *A material gain.*
4. *A feeling of comfort.*

So that's what this first chapter is all about: How to use your supervisory and managerial skills to satisfy your employees' desires while they're on the job so they'll in turn work as hard as they can for your benefit.

And that's the law of reversal. You see, in its simplest terms, *the law of reversal is give to get.* If you want to get ahead, you have to forget your own selfish interests and serve the interests of others. Do that, and you'll get returns automatically through the law of reversal.

Right there you have the basic reason why the law of reversal is so little understood by so many people! 95 percent of the people can't believe that *you must give to get.* 95 percent of the population think that you can't give before you get. But the successful 5 percent know that *you must give before you can get!*

The heart that gives freely, obtains in abundance.

This old proverb is one of Bob Gallivan's favorites, and rightly so. Bob practiced the law of reversal so well that he was earning more money in one year *in his twenties* than a lot of men earn in 5 to 10 years!

"The salesman who thinks only about his commission—about how much money he'll make on every sale—is destined for failure for he's thinking only of himself," Bob says. "The successful salesman is interested in helping his customer—in giving him the best service possible. That salesman is bound to succeed; he can't miss for he's practicing the law of reversal."

You can read about Bob's spectacular success in his book, *How I Started Earning $50,000 a year in sales at the age of 26.* It's published by Prentice-Hall, Inc.

Englewood Cliffs, New Jersey, and features Mr. Gallivan's amazing Give-and-Get Method.

The Strangest Secret.

Earl Nightingale, the famous Chicago radio commentator for Station WGN in the fifties, understood the law of give to get better than most. He retired at the age of 35 with an income of over $30,000 a year! Mr. Nightingale, in his Columbia recording, *The Strangest Secret,* in effect, says this about the law of reversal.

"Out of every 100 men who start out even, only 5 will make the financial grade by the time they're 65! One of those 5 will be rich; 4 will be financially independent. Of the 59 others who are still living, 5 will still be working—54 will be broke! And all because they get the cart before the horse. Those 59 think that you have to get before you can give; the 5 successful men know that you must give before you can get!"

The law of success.

You might also be interested in knowing that the *law of success* uses the same principle as the *law of reversal.* Few people realize that, however. Most people think that if you make a lot of money, you're successful. That's not true at all. *Success is not the result of making money; making money is the result of success!* And your success will be in direct proportion to your service. Again, simply said—you must give to get.

Every man has certain goals in life.

Remember that every single individual who works for you has certain goals—certain objectives in life—that he wants to attain. What are these goals? Well, of course, they vary; they're slightly different with each one of us since our personal tastes are so different. But there's one thing you can be sure of, and it's this:

Each and every one of us wants to know how to be loved, how to win fame or fortune or power, and how to stay healthy!

Write your own ticket!

In other words, if you can show a man how to be richer, smarter, healthier, lazier, sexier, or more important—you can write your own ticket! If all of us want these things out of life, where lies the difference in us then? Why not treat each man the same way? Well, here's at least part of the difference.

Each one of us has a different concept of which one of these goals is more important in our lives, and even a different idea of what represents each goal.

Although the goal in itself is *objective,* a person's viewpoint of it will be entirely *subjective.* Some people, for example, would get a feeling of security from money, a fat bank account, and a big life insurance policy; others—from a position where there is a good relationship with the boss and one's associates—that sort of thing.

Even recreation . . . .

Just take such a simple matter as recreation. I like to bowl and play golf. Some men like to fish and hunt. Others are swimming and boating enthusiasts. Some enjoy only the spectator sports—baseball, football, etc. One spectator sport even has a theme song: *music to watch girls by.* But all of us have one goal in mind—recreation, play, leisure. However, our methods of obtaining that goal—our own self-satisfaction—are all completely different.

You must find the right approach.

The smart supervisor always tries to find the best approach to use with each individual. For instance, well-timed praise can spur one person on to even greater heights of achievement, while it may only inflate another's ego. One in a million might be embarrassed by your praise.

Criticism can turn some people sour and bitter, but it may also be so embarrassing to others that they'll strive to do better for you. You must know and be able to judge each one of your people if you want to properly supervise and control them to get the best results from them.

I want you to look again at the four desires a person spends most of his money on and see how your helping him get them on the job will benefit you. I'll also tell you what techniques you can use to help him get them. So let me list these four desires for you once more—

1. *A feeling of security.*
2. *A feeling of pride or satisfaction of one's ego.*
3. *A material gain.*
4. *A feeling of comfort.*

Good salesmen use these four desires to sell their customers, too.

A good salesman knows that these four desires are the four main reasons people buy anything. So look at them for a moment from the reverse side—from the side of the salesman. True enough, some of the sales consultants and the sales engineers will try to give you a lot of other technical classroom reasons why people spend their money, but when *the biggest retailer in all the world*—Sears Roebuck, boils them down to these four, that's good enough for me!

How to use these four principles of salesmanship in your supervision.

Why is this so important to you? What does it have to do with the secrets of dynamic supervision? How will you benefit by knowing and applying these four principles of good salesmanship to your own daily supervisory problems? Well, here's how they'll help you:

Since this list represents *the four main ways people spend their money* to gain satisfaction for themselves *off the job*—why not give them these same four basic items *on the job?* Do that—and they'll be all the more satisfied with their work. And the more satisfied they are with their jobs—the more satisfied they'll be with you, and the harder they'll work for you.

Tie a string to them.

So if you'll make these items—*security, gain, pride, comfort*—available to your employees on the job (with a string attached so that their attainment is dependent upon their performance) they'll work just that much harder to get them. See now how you can benefit in your supervision and control of others by applying the four basic principles of good salesmanship?

Use as many of them as you can at a time.

Incidentally, a top-notch salesman tries to use all four of these benefits when he's trying to turn a prospect into a customer, but he's happy if he can plug at least two of them. So for our purposes here, *security, pride, and gain will be the three mainstays;* the fourth one—*comfort,* we'll let go by the boards. That should be a built-in benefit for all your employees, anyway, *with no strings attached.* Here's how you can give your employees—

1. A feeling of security on the job.

The best example of perfect security is often said to be a man serving a life sentence in prison, but that's the complete opposite of what you want. You want your employees to have the *security of opportunity, approval, advancement, promotion, recognition, self-respect, and self-reliance.* If you can offer your employees this kind of security, they can concentrate on *how to do a better job for you* instead of just concentrating on keeping their jobs.

It happens to executives, too.

A New York psychiatrist, Dr. Abraham Jacobson, says that insecurity in one's job can lead to peptic ulcers, cardiac flutter, alcoholism, and even severe mental illness. "It isn't the actual salary in dollars and cents that an executive is often concerned with," Dr. Jacobson says. "It's the question in his mind when he goes home on Friday whether he'll still have his job on Monday. His position can be wiped out over the weekend in some reorganization of the company. One high-powered top-salaried executive told me, 'I never go into my office on Monday morning before I check the name on the door. I never know for sure what might have happened over the weekend while I was gone!' "

A situation like that doesn't make for security and peace of mind at all. It makes for nothing but insecurity and fear. If you want to establish good long-term, friendly-yet-firm relationships with your employees, don't count on using fear and insecurity as your aids!

Four specific methods to give a man security and peace of mind.

In addition to money, promotion, advancement, reward, and the like, security can be given to your employees in four other exact ways. Here's what you can do to give your people peace of mind so they can concentrate on giving you peak performance:

    a. *Let your men know why they're where they are.*
    b. *Make him feel that he belongs where he is.*
    c. *Place him in a job for which he's been properly trained.*
    d. *Let him know how his efforts fit into the big picture.*

a. Let him know why he's there.

It's readily understandable for a soldier to ask, "What am I doing here? Is this trip really necessary?" In these United States with our policy of a civilian type military structure, answering this question for a draftee who'd rather be anywhere else than in uniform is a challenge for all of the armed forces. Often it's just as hard to answer this question in business and industry. A man can be a square peg in a round hole out here as well as in there.

b. If he doesn't feel that he belongs — he won't stay!

Not too long ago, one of the giants in the electronics industry built a branch plant in a flourishing Midwestern city. They had a requirement for a work force of nearly 3,500 men. This company had no desire to bleed other industrial firms in the area of their skilled employees; in fact, they bent over backward trying to avoid hiring them—but in many cases, it happened anyway.

"Evidently I didn't make my employees feel they really belonged where they were when they worked for me," one worried plant manager said. "They left me to go to work for this new outfit for less money than I was paying them! I know for a fact that in some cases I was paying my men 32 cents an hour more, and still—they left me!

"So money's not the total answer!" he went on to say. "It's important, sure, but it's not everything. I know that now, but I'm still trying to explain what happened to the president and the board of directors up in Chicago. When you have to curtail your operations right in the middle of an expansion program, that takes some tall explaining, let me tell you!

"We have a brand-new program in our plant now headed up by our industrial relations manager and we're making an extra special effort to make our men feel that they belong with us. And that's orders from headquarters. Brother, I just can't afford any more manpower losses like that last one!"

I'm sure you'll understand why I've not mentioned any names here, but let this point sink in, if you will, please. *There are very few drives of a man stronger than his desire to be identified with some group of people.*

When you let a man know that he's wanted, that he has a definite spot in your company, a specific job to do, and that his efforts are contributing to the achievement of a common goal, you've got a man who'll have pride in himself, his fellow employees, his superiors, and his company! Getting him to feel that way is up to you. If you can do it, you can bet he'll stick with you. He'll not run away the moment a new company opens up next door.

c. Place him in a job for which he's been properly trained.

"Union restrictions can sometimes tie your hands on this if you don't learn to work with your local," says Frank Hanson of Western Electric. "But the local union president and I both keep right on top of this situation all the time so that the reassignment of any man takes into consideration the desires of the man, the welfare of the whole union, and the accomplishment of the mission for management. We try to help each other—not to cut the other fellow's throat!"

Keep two central points in mind here. Give a man a job that's too big for him and he'll end up a discontented and frustrated individual; give him one that's too small and you'll have the same end results. *Always match the man and his abilities to the job that's to be done.*

Meet a true professional who knows how to do it.

Red Schoendist, one of the finest players and managers baseball has ever known, had this to say about the importance of knowing his men when he was pilot for the St. Louis Cardinals.

"I don't criticize my men very much," he said. "It's easy to criticize, but I played this game, too, and I know it isn't all that simple. So all I ask of them is just that they hustle and play hard.

"That's why the most important part of managing is knowing your players," Red went on to say. "Each man doesn't have the same amount of talent and you have to know your players and what they can do."

d. Let a man know he's important in the big picture.

Each man must feel that he's important in his position, that he's doing something worthwhile. I don't care what his job is, you must lend dignity and respect to it. He must realize that it takes a lot of cogs to make up a wheel, and that even a *big wheel* won't turn properly when one of the smallest cogs is broken.

2. Appeal to a man's pride — to his ego.

The second principle of good salesmanship is to appeal to a man's pride—to help him satisfy his ego. It's also one of the most valuable tools you can use to motivate a man to do his best for you. There's a great deal of desire for praise in each one of us, and few things can be more motivating to an employee than recognition and reward for a job well done.

Give a man recognition of some sort.

Remember the thoughts of Mr. Meyer, if you will, that a man will work hard to gain the *recognition of others.* That recognition may be nothing more than a pat on the back, a word of praise and encouragement, an appreciative letter, or it may be a bonus in the pay envelope, perhaps a promotion.

The recognition you give should be out of the ordinary routine run of things, but you shouldn't emphasize it to the point of embarrassment as if you were doing the man a favor. Don't obligate him to do something for you in return. Keep it on a businesslike basis. Or, as Kin Hubbard so aptly put it once, "Don't pay a man a compliment like you expected a receipt for it!"

Pride can take some rather odd forms at times. When a woman slaves away to clean up her house so it'll be ready for the cleaning woman when she comes—that's pride! When your stomach flips over at the sight of your secretary yawning and looking bored as she proofreads the latest supersonic management-labor-relations letter you've just dictated—that's pride, too—in reverse!

Remember though, whatever form it takes, recognition of a man's efforts is a valuable supervisory tool too often neglected by management in the hustle and bustle of getting the job done. Always appeal to a man's pride, to his sense of honor, and you'll motivate him to do his best when nothing else can stir him.

3. Offer a man material gain.

The third basic principle of salesmanship is to *offer a man a material gain.* (A material gain is often represented as a *saving* by the salesman.) Now it's true enough that a lot of us will respond to a kind word or a compliment, and we usually respond immediately, but often it's only a temporary response.

You can't dry today's wash with yesterday's sun, and that's why a material gain is so effective; it's felt on every payday. Oh, you'll hear a few people say that money's not that important, but I feel this way about it. Maybe money's not the most important thing in the world, but I know one thing for sure; it's running a hot second to whatever is first!

And money's the only way we can really measure a man's success or failure in this materialistic world we live in. The President and Congress are always concerned about the cost-of-living index, the national budget, the gross national product, and poverty, too; in fact, they're interested in everything that has to do with your money.

Let's face it. You can't buy a house or a car or a boat by compliments alone. A good salesman will appreciate your kind words—but he needs your cold hard cash to make a sale!

Five guidelines to use.

Here, you can use five definite guidelines to help direct a man's financial progress on the job. You can stimulate your employees to do a better job and to earn more money by—
1. *Using competition.*
2. *Rewarding success.*
3. *Punishing failure.*
4. *Promotion and advancement.*
5. *Incentives and bonuses.*

Money makes the mare go.

Let's not kid ourselves; money makes the mare go. If we didn't need money, we wouldn't work, would we? I know I wouldn't. Of course, it's far better if you can earn your daily dollars at a job you like, but like it or not—you still have to earn that almighty dollar every day to live.

The difference between an amateur and a professional is — money!

An amateur writer may be proud of his article or his story; so is the professional. What's the big difference? *Money!* The professional gets paid for writing. He gets the joy of the amateur and coin of the realm, too. Even the old master, William Somerset Maugham, said that he wrote for money. And Hemingway was not at all bashful about being paid for his work.

Russell Conwell, the founder and first president of Temple University, was also the pastor of Philadelphia's famed Baptist Temple. He was often criticized by others for advocating that it was a man's Christian duty to make as much money as he *honestly* could. He used to answer his critics this way: "To make money honestly is to preach the gospel. You don't have to be poor to be pious!"

And you don't have to be a Mr. Meyer or a Russell Conwell to gain the benefits of having employees who will—

1. *Respect and have confidence in you.*
2. *Gladly give you their willing obedience,*
   their loyal cooperation, and their wholehearted support.
3. *Work with initiative, ingenuity, and enthusiasm.*
4. *Work together as a team with high spirit, morale,*
   and esprit with direction and purpose toward a common goal.
5. *Feel that they belong where they are—with you!*
6. *Work as hard as they can to make a profit—for you!*

All you have to do to get these six benefits is practice the first three of the four basic principles of salesmanship by using the *law of reversal*. The fourth one—*comfort*—should be built into your organization already. Make an effort to offer your employees a

1. *Feeling of safety or security.*
2. *Feeling of pride or satisfaction of their ego.*
3. *Material gain.*

To sum it all up.

To sum it all up, let me say that since a feeling of *security* is one of the prime movers in most people, giving *recognition* to your employees by a bonus, an incentive, a promotion, or some other tangible *material gain* is a good way to get them to put forth with their best efforts for you. Right here in one stroke you've satisfied three of their four main desires.

THE 2ND SECRET

How to Use the Silent Skill

Do you want to find out what's going on in your own department? *Then listen to your employees with an open mind.* Do you want your men to like you? All you have to do is to *let them talk to you* about their personal problems, their worries, their fears. Do you want a man to tell you the truth—to level with you? *Then give him the courtesy of listening* to what he has to say. To listen carefully and attentively is one of the highest compliments you can pay anyone.

Here are just a few of the advantages that will accrue to you when you learn how to *practice the silent skill* properly.

1. *Your employees will not only accept you,*
   they'll even like you when you listen to them.
2. *When you encourage a man to talk freely about himself*
   and his problems, you'll get to know and to understand him better.
3. *Listening lets your subordinate know that you're*
   really interested in him.
4. *Listen to what he says, and you'll learn a lot about*
   your own shop by listening "between the lines" to what
   he didn't say!
5. *Want to be successful? One of the hallmarks of a successful*
   executive is that "he listens." And success is a definite advantage
   for you to gain. Am I right?

Allen Weatherly learned to listen "the hard way."

"The best thing that ever happened to me was getting my jaw broken," says Allen Weatherly of Pacific Gas and Electric. "I was a green line supervisor for P G & E, fresh out of college with my engineering degree, and of course, I thought I knew it all.

"I even went so far as to tell old-timers how to climb poles and they'd been doing it long before I was born. I wouldn't listen to anyone. But how could I? My own mouth was always open! Then luckily, I broke my jaws in a car accident; I had to wear a cast for three months. Couldn't say a word; all I could do was mumble.

"So I had no choice. I had to listen to others. And did I learn? Whew! My ears burned for a while, let me tell you. My men really poured it on thick and fast and they loved it for I couldn't talk back! Of course I knew later on they did it for my own good, but I didn't think so then.

"Whatever success I've had, I credit it primarily to the fact that I was forced to learn the difficult art of listening—and then, only by accident! For my money, *the silent skill is one of the finest supervisory tools you've got in your kit* if you'll just use it properly. My advice to young foremen and young supervisors who want to get ahead is very simple: *Just listen to your men. Listen—listen—and then listen some more!"*

That advice sounds simple enough, doesn't it? True enough, it is—in a way. Using the silent skill is *simple*—but it's *not easy*. Don't confuse simple with easy. They're not the same at all. It's oh-so-simple to say, "Listen to your men!" But far too many times, it's not easy to do. You've got to work at it.

Listening takes a lot of effort.

Believe it or not, listening is actually hard work. You can burn up more calories and energy in four hours of solid listening than you will in eight hours of hard physical labor. When you listen intently, your body activities speed up.

Your heart beats faster; the blood circulates more rapidly. There's a slight rise in body temperature; respiration and oxygen intake increase. Why? Because listening requires an actual physical effort on your part. More adrenalin is pumped into your blood stream. Your body becomes more tense; muscles contract. You concentrate harder on what you're trying to hear, to understand, and to absorb.

Silence is a sedative.

Ever find yourself getting jumpy and on edge, nervous and irritable for no reason at all? Suddenly you're screaming at your children, or you're yelling at your wife at the top of your voice. They turn down the television set or the record player so they can hear you, and immediately—your irritation is completely gone! That's all that was wrong with you—too much noise! *Silence is a better sedative than aspirin can ever hope to be.*

This is a noisy world we live in, and there's no indication that it's going to get any quieter. We're distracted not only by what we hear, but also, by what we see. A poor listener will be easily influenced by every distraction, even in an extremely intimate face-to-face situation.

Get rid of distractions.

A good listener will always take steps to get rid of the distractions. Sometimes it's easily done, for example—by closing a door, shutting off a radio, turning down the television set, going into another room, moving closer to the person who's talking, or asking him to speak a little louder.

If you can't get rid of these distractions by any of these methods, then it becomes a matter of intense concentration for you. And the harder you have to concentrate on actually hearing the person, the harder it'll be for you to understand and absorb what he's trying to get across to you. The harder you listen—the more irritable you'll become. If you don't think that's true—

Try this experiment tonight when you get home.

Turn on every electrical appliance you've got in your house that makes noise and there are a lot of them. Turn on the radio, the television set, the record player, the washing machine, the dryer, the dishwasher, the garbage disposal, the kitchen exhaust fan, and the vacuum cleaner. If you have more than I've mentioned, turn them on, too, but I assure you these are enough.

Now ask your wife and your children to start a good healthy argument right in front of you while you sit down and try to reconcile your check stubs with the monthly bank statement. If you can last five minutes without blowing your stack, you're a far better man than I am!

Keep the communication lines open.

You can make all this hard work a lot easier for yourself by using these six words to keep the communication lines open. If you can learn to ask—

1. *Who*—
  2. *What*—
    3. *When*—
      4. *Where*—
        5. *Why*—
          6. *How*—

at the right time, you're well on your way to success in developing your skills in the difficult *art of listening*.

And that's what I want you to get out of this chapter. How to ask questions that will cause your subordinate to talk about himself and his problems. I'll show you how to get the benefits I told you about in the beginning by giving you some definite guidelines to follow in your questioning techniques.

I'll tell you what good questions ought to do, and I'll give you the characteristics of a good question. Finally, I'll give you a few questions so you can check yourself out on your own listening abilities. Then I'll recap it all for you in a nutshell at the end. Before I do that, though, I want you to know

How to decide which employees to listen to.

I can answer that very simply by saying, "All of them, including the janitor!" You say you don't have time? Well, just remember this. First of all, you don't have to listen to all of them at the same time. Secondly, remember that good profit making ideas can come from the most unlikely places. Millionaires got that way not only by plowing their own brain furrows, but by cultivating a lot of other people's, too!

You need use only four words to turn your most reluctant employee into a potential political candidate. Just ask, "What is your opinion?" That's all you need to say. Then turn on your pocket tape recorder, light up a long cigar, and sit back and relax.

Here's how to have employees who'll accept you and like you, too.

Besides asking *who, what, when, where, why and how* to stimulate your employee to talk about himself, you can use other techniques to gain the benefit of having subordinates who will accept you and like you when you listen to them.

In the first place, when you practice the silent skill, you can get rid of one of the problems all young supervisors face. It's the "I'll make 'em like me by being sweet and nice, using soft-soap and babying them along" idea.

You see, when you ask *who, what, when, where, why, and how*—you're not being sweet and pleasant at all. These questions are as hard as nails. They're tough to answer for they're direct and to the point. They don't give any room for evasion or deviation. You're using them to get your men to talk so you can learn from them.

And it's just plain old human nature for them to like you when you listen to them. Have you ever disliked a person who listened intently to your ideas or your opinions? Or let me ask you this way: Have you ever liked someone who wouldn't listen to your viewpoints at all? I said in the beginning, and it's well worth repeating here; to give a speaker your rapt attention is to pay him one of your highest compliments.

For example, I've heard it said, and I truly believe it, that many a person calls a doctor when all he wants is a sympathetic ear. In fact, a sympathetic ear is often the way a woman cures all her sorrows. I'm not a marriage counselor, but if you happen to be having marital problems, you might give it a try. It's a lot cheaper than Reno and alimony payments for the rest of your life.

What good questions will do for you.

1. Questioning your men will stimulate their thinking.

Whenever you get right down to specifics by asking who, what, when, where, why, and how, your employee is forced to give concrete and direct answers. This is especially true if the question is directed toward some phase of his work.

2. Questioning will give your employees a chance to express their own ideas.

You can find out by questioning—*and then by listening to the answer*—what the attitudes of your employees are about the plant, your department, their superiors, their fellow workers. Getting them to talk first about their work is a good way of getting them to talk about themselves next.

3. Asking questions is the only reliable way to get accurate information.

Never dominate a conversation by doing all the talking yourself if you want to find out where your people stand on a certain point. Take a lesson from the efficiency experts. They always ask painful and pointed questions and they listen carefully to the answers. I have yet to hear one answer a single question—about his progress, at any rate—until it's time for his final report. So work like an efficiency expert; ask questions and then listen to the answer. To get information, all you have to do is to insert another question whenever the man stops talking. Just prime the pump; let him work the handle.

Characteristics of a good question.

Well phrased questions are the key to good sound questioning techniques. A good question should cover these six points.

1. It should have a specific purpose.

Your questions should be designed for definite purposes. One question might be used to emphasize a major point, another to stimulate thought, and yet another to arouse interest and make your men more alert. If you yourself will ask, "Are there any questions?", you'll give your men the opportunity to clear up any misunderstandings and they can voice their own opinions.

2. It must be understood by all your men.

Questions should be phrased in language and terms that are familiar to all your employees. Your questions should be worded in such a way that your listener will have no trouble in understanding exactly what you want. If your question creates another question in your listener's mind, it's useless. "Please tell me exactly what you want me to do," is an age-old plea of employees to their supervisors.

3. It should emphasize only one point at a time.

Avoid asking two questions in one or asking a question in such a way that several other questions are needed to understand the first one or to bring out the information that you want. Don't scatter your fire. The words, "This *one* thing I do," are as valid today as when the Apostle Paul wrote them to the Philippians nearly two thousand years ago.

4. A good question asks for a definite answer.

Don't let your men bluff you or get away with vague nonspecific answers that tell you nothing. State your question in such a way that a definite answer will be required, and don't give up until you get it.

5. It should discourage guessing.

Never word your questions in such a way that your listener can guess at an answer and satisfy you. His answer should be based on information and facts, not imagination and fancy. There'll be times when you'll be asking for his candid opinion, but subjective thinking has to be based upon objective facts.

6. The best question always asks "Why?"

The *why* can be either spoken or implied, but it should always be there. Too many supervisors are content with an answer of *yes* or *no,* even when that answer tells them nothing. If a man says "Yes," ask him *why;* if he says "No," ask him *why.* If he says it's always been done this way before, ask him *why.* That little three-letter word is one of the most potent question words you can use.

Listening to problems is a management responsibility.

Listening to the problems of your men is one of the responsibilities of management. It begins at the level of the front-line supervisor. If you, as a supervisor or an executive of management, won't listen—*the labor union will!* You'll find out how to listen the hard way when labor files a grievance or when it's time to write a new contract.

Not long ago, I had the opportunity to review the points a certain labor union wanted written into its new contract with the company. The union was satisfied with all the proposals of management when it came to wages, hours, incentive payments, vacations, retirement, and all the other fringe benefits.

But they went out on strike and refused to renew their contract because of one specific point. *They wanted a better grievance procedure.* In the past, problems presented by the men to management dragged on for months without solution. In some cases, the grievances had even been thrown away and could not be found!

"The management is not concerned with the problems of our men," the local union president told me. "The employees are more than satisfied with the wage offer and other benefits presented to them by the company, but they want a better grievance procedure, and they won't go back to work until they get it!"

Ford listens, too.

"I can tell you immediately what's wrong when one of the men in the plant asks to see me about a personal problem," says George Watson, industrial relations manager with one of Ford's assembly plants. "He's got a supervisor who thinks he's either too busy or too important to listen to a subordinate's troubles.

"I always talk to the man first, and afterward—to the supervisor. When the man is in my office—I listen; when the supervisor comes in, then it's my turn—*he listens*!"

And if Ford can spare the time to listen—so can you!

How you can turn an angry employee into a satisfied one just by listening.

As I just said, listening to a man's problems is a distinct responsibility of management, but doing it properly takes a special bit of tact and a definite technique. Listen to how Jack Wood, one of Dow Chemical's top employee relations men, handles a recalcitrant employee.

"First of all, *you've got to listen to the man's story from beginning to end without saying a single word,*" says Mr. Wood. "Don't interrupt him, not even once! Let him get it off his chest. That's the first thing he wants. Somebody who'll listen patiently to him; someone who'll give him a sympathetic ear.

"Next, after he's finished, *agree with him,* even if you don't! Remember that you're management so you're probably biased, too. Tell him you understand completely how he feels about this problem, and that if you were in his shoes, you'd probably look at it the same way. *You've got to see it from his point of view.*

"You've taken a lot of the fire out of him by first *listening* to him, and second, by *agreeing* with him. You can bet he wasn't prepared for that. And now, you add the finishing touch by *asking him what he wants you to do about it.*

"You know he wasn't at all prepared for that last one. Ninety-nine out of every one hundred management men *tell* a man what they're going to do for him. You can't win his support that way. *Don't tell him what you're going to do; ask him what he wants you to do!*

"I've had men look at me in astonishment and say, 'Sir, I really don't know. Nothing, I guess. I just wanted someone to listen to my side of the story. You've done that so I guess that's all. I'm satisfied.'

"They leave, completely satisfied with *the answer I didn't give them.* You see, they supplied their own answer. All they wanted was someone to sympathize with them; to feel sorry for them. And that's all I did.

"What does that cost? Nothing," Jack says in conclusion. "I'm being paid for keeping good management-employee relations in the plant. Does it pay off for us? You figure it out. Of course, we've no way of knowing how many acts of sabotage it's stopped, or how many wildcat strikes it's prevented. But we can get a good idea by looking at the records of other companies."

In summary then, here's all you have to do:
1. *Listen to a man's story from beginning to end without saying a single word.*
   2. *Agree with him from his point of view.*
      3. *Ask him what he wants you to do about it.*

You have to kick the conversation in gear.

You can get a man to talk freely about himself and his problems if you'll follow the pointers I gave you about questioning techniques. But it's still your responsibility to initiate the conversation. Do that and you won't encounter this problem:

"Too many times a supervisor and his men go around just staring at each other," says Fred Barton, a production superintendent with United States Steel. "They act much like a couple of strange dogs sniffing at each other, just waiting to see who'll give ground first. Naturally, the subordinate is hesitant to talk unless his supervisor says something first.

"I've found the best way to get a fellow started is to ask him a question. Any question; I don't care what it is. Ask him what time it is; that's at least a start. Just ask him something to get his mouth open for you."

And I agree, although it's much better if you can use specific questions that will keep your man talking. You see, the best and fastest way to get to know your people is to encourage them to talk freely, without any fear of ridicule or disapproval.

Listen between the lines.

A great many times you can learn more by what your subordinate didn't say than by what he did say. *So listen between the lines.* Just because he didn't say that he dislikes his supervisor isn't any sign that he likes him. The speaker doesn't always put everything that he's thinking into words. Not only that, watch for the changing tone and volume of his voice. You'll often find a meaning that's in direct contrast to his words. Watch his facial expression, his mannerisms, his gestures, the movements of his body. To be a good listener requires that you *use your eyes as well as your ears.*

Check yourself out with these.

Here are a few questions you can use to check yourself out on your own listening abilities.

1. Do you make it easy for employees to talk to you?

You don't have to be overly chummy nor do you have to be cold, distant, and standoffish. Just ask a few simple leading questions. That's the easy way. There's no opposing lawyer facing you here to object to your leading questions. They're quite proper.

2. Are you sympathetic with your employee's problems?

Maybe you've got problems of your own, too. Susie needs braces on her teeth; personal property taxes are due next month; car needs some new tires and a tune-up job. Problems and more problems. The point is that your employees aren't concerned with your problems. They're not getting paid to worry about you; *you're getting paid to worry about them.* So lend them a sympathetic ear. Do that and they'll stand up and fight for you.

3. Do you encourage suggestions and ideas from your people?

If you don't, you haven't learned how to use the silent skill yet. Brush-off a man just once. Interrupt him—don't let him talk, and he'll never use his ingenuity for you again. From then on, he'll be deader than all the machinery in your plant.

4. Do you make an effort to improve yourself in human relations?

This is the best way to start: listening to your subordinates; using the silent skill. A good listener is not only popular everywhere, but after a while, he even knows something. If you want to impress others with your knowledge, stimulate them to talk all the time. Ask them a couple of questions about themselves and they're off and running.

They'll always think of you as being such an interesting fellow to talk with; a scintillating conversationalist! And you can build that enviable reputation without ever saying a single word.

5. Do you make an extra effort to remember names and faces?

You can if you'll just *stop, look, and listen.* You can't if you're too busy telling others about your own exploits. If you want others to know how good you are—*let your boss tell them!* It'll carry a lot more weight.

In a nutshell . . . .

Let me put it in a nutshell for you now right here. First of all, think again of the benefits that can be yours when you learn how to use the silent skill.

1. *You'll have people who'll like you and accept you for listening to them.*
2. *You'll know your people better, and you'll understand them better when you get them to talk freely about themselves and their problems.* (By the way, did I remember to mention that things that are problems at labor's level become responsibilities at management's level?)

3. *You'll have people who know that you're really interested in*
   them, and so—they'll be interested in you!
   4. *You'll be able to find out what's going on in your own shop by listening*
      "between the lines." You can learn more about your operation in a few
      minutes from an employee than you can from a written
      report in a few hours.
      5. *You'll become successful, for one of the hallmarks of a succes*
         supervisor is that "he listens."

And how do you get these benefits? By learning how to ask good, solid, specific
questions that have the elements of—

who,

   what,

      when,

         where,

            why,

               how in them to get a direct concrete answer from your employees.
Then *listen—listen—and listen some more!*

How to Build a Superior Outfit —
with Ordinary Men

What are some of the advantages of having a superior outfit? I doubt if there are enough pages in this book, let alone in this chapter, to discuss fully all the benefits of having a top-notch organization.

I know what some of them are, though. You'll enjoy such benefits as a deep and full friendship with your employees. You'll understand them better, and you'll be able to develop a rich and rewarding relationship with them when you do. That's a concrete and specific benefit that no amount of money can buy. I've known industrial managers and business executives who'd give their shirt to develop such a harmonious rapport with their subordinates, but they can't. They simply don't know how!

When you have a superior outfit, you'll have increased organizational efficiency that runs all the way from the front door to the back door; from your personnel and administrative sections through your production lines on out to your packing and shipping departments. With a peak performance throughout your plant, you'll enjoy increased profits, too.

Not only that, there'll also be that intangible, but highly important, matter of pride; that same kind of pride you feel when you say you're proud of your son, your school, your team, your regiment, your department, or your plant. Yes, you'll be proud of your employees, for you'll feel a deep and rich satisfaction in their accomplishments.

In short, the achievement of building a top-notch outfit with but the ordinary run of manpower makes life worth living; it's a constant daily challenge to your abilities.

Here's how Jim Henderson makes it work.

So that you can get a better grasp of the real and tangible advantages of having a superior outfit, I thought it would be best for me to get hold of Jim Henderson, the head of a highly successful and prominent St. Louis general contracting firm, so he could tell you exactly what building a top-notch company from just ordinary and average men has meant to him. I drove up to St. Louis the other day to have lunch with Jim and to talk with him again. Here's what he told me.

"It's hard for me to tell you all the benefits that I've enjoyed from building a superior company up from scratch," said Jim. "Sure, I've gained many material benefits; that's why most of us work, anyway, although after you reach a certain level, money becomes less important—except to the tax collector, of course!

"But after you reach that point, it's the challenge of the job that makes it worthwhile. It's sort of like asking a man why he climbs a mountain. He does it just because it's there; he climbs the mountain simply to see if he can do it. Business presents the same challenge; I want to see if I can do it, too!

"If money alone were my goal, I'd have quit long ago," Jim said. "But it's not. Just look at that." He turned from our table to point out the window at the beautiful Gateway Arch, the pride of St. Louis. "What an engineering achievement. What I'd have given to have been chosen for that job!" He turned back with a sigh of regret and a sheepish grin. "See what I mean about money not being everything? It's the challenge of the job that's important, too. Oh, well; back to business!"

There are four basic principles for you to follow.

"There are four basic principles to use if you want to create a superior outfit," Jim went on to say. "Maybe it would be more accurate to say there are four facts that you must accept as being valid before you start. And then you must act upon them before you can raise your company to its maximum production potential. Here's what they are:

"*First, the superior outfit must be created from the ordinary and average run of manpower.*

"Before I give you the second principle, and so that you will fully understand it, you should know that the men who work for you will fall into three basic broad groups based on their general abilities and talents. There's a comparatively small upper group, a large middle group, and another rather small lower group. Keeping these facts in mind, then, let me give you that second principle, which is—

"*The superiority of your outfit depends upon your ability to bring the men of the lower group up to that level of skill and proficiency where they will become an asset to your entire organizational effort.*

"*The third principle in this: All your employees must want to do what you want them to do.*

"Far too many employers don't understand this principle. Most of them think only in terms of their employees *having to do* what the boss wants them to do. That's the wrong approach. The key to this third principle is getting your employees to *want to do* what you want them to do. If they don't want to carry out your orders, or if they don't want to do what you desire, you haven't properly motivated them. You'll never build a superior outfit until you do.

"*Fourth, and last. The top outfit, the really superior outfit, is always the one who is better in ALL THINGS than anyone else!*

"Those are the four principles that I feel are absolutely essential to follow before you can build a superior outfit with ordinary people. And I know this much for sure; it can be done!"

I must agree wholeheartedly with Jim. After all, he picked up the luncheon check. Truthfully though, between the two of us we figured out what these principles were in determining the reasons for the success of his company. Jim knew in general what they were. My main contribution was helping him to get them down in black and white.

Now I want to use the rest of this chapter to discuss these four basic principles in some detail and to show you some techniques you can use to make them work. So from the top down again—

1. The superior outfit must be created from the ordinary and average run of manpower.

Do you accept this idea? It's true, isn't it? Ever hear a military man reminisce about his years in service, especially the combat years? He's quite a dreamer, really; he's an expert in the art of verbal fictioneering. "Why, if I could just have that First Sergeant I had in France in World War II," he says. "Or if I had that young Captain I met in Korea; and that operations officer who served with me in Vietnam, and . . . . Man, if I could just have all those guys together at one time, what an outfit I could build!"

Despite their propaganda, Marines are made from ordinary men, too!

I've never been a Marine, but I'm sure that most of them were just ordinary and average men, at least, until they got in the Marine Corps and were told differently by their press agent! I have a brother-in-law who must have been briefed by a supersonic public relations officer. He still thinks all Marines are related to Superman in one way or another. And he was in the Corps for only three years in World War II! He hasn't had a uniform on for over 20 years now, but he was so well indoctrinated that to this day he considers himself to be a Marine! Warren Kelly, I salute you!

Marines can create superior outfits from ordinary men, too.

Speaking of Marines, I can tell you about one outfit that built a superior unit—with just ordinary and average men. And that was the 1st Marine Division.

That famous division had to fight its way back in December 1950 from the Chosin Reservoir to the south through hordes of attacking Chinese Communists. It was joined in battle with the enemy from the moment the column struck its camp at Hagaru. By midnight, after suffering heavy losses throughout the day, it had bivouacked at Kotori, still surrounded by the enemy and still far from the sea and safety.

The Division Commander, Major General Oliver P. Smith, was alone in his tent. It was his darkest moment. The task lying ahead seemed hopeless—a lost cause. It seemed impossible to get his men to the sea and the safety of the rescue ships. But suddenly above the noise of the wind and the enemy gunfire, he heard music. Outside his tent some Marines were singing the Marine Corps Hymn.

"Their raw courage struck me to the quick," General Smith said. "All doubt left me. I knew then we had it made. *These men were Marines!*"

Adversity creates superiority.

Adversity had welded these men into a superior outfit. They refused to be defeated! I've heard it said that man's extremity is God's opportunity. So don't quit when the going gets tough. Anyone can succeed at an easy task. It takes courage and perseverance to come through when the odds are all stacked against you.

I know that out here in civilian life you and I don't have the opportunity to make headlines the way a military man does. At any rate, we don't face the adversities he does, and as a result, our victories are seldom found on the front page. Maybe they're less flamboyant, but they're still victories. We may not get any medals for our exploits, but we don't have to duck any bullets either!

But even in civilian life, you still have to start with ordinary and average men to build your superior outfit. Usually, to get employees, you put an ad in the paper which says, in essence, "Wanted—good men . . . good wages . . ." and depending upon how badly you need employees and how tight the labor market is, you're going to get the run of the mill—from the top to the bottom—just plain ordinary people. No Einsteins; no Baruchs; no geniuses. Just people named Smith and Brown and Jones—and Van Fleet and Van der Zee, too, along with Sloditski and Murphy and McClenahan. Maybe even some Wongs and Obayashis, too.

You must concentrate on one man at a time.

Creating a superior outfit is basically the task of raising each employee's individual performance to a level that is satisfactory to you. Some will require more time and patience and polish than others. *But you've got to start with the individual.*

Get each man and woman to do their level best.

"Whenever you see a company or a corporation that's a leader in their field, an outfit that's on top of the profit ladder, be sure to remember one thing," says Barney Owens, personnel manager for United Electric in Rockford, Illinois. "They don't have any superhumans working for them. No sir; they have plain and ordinary average citizens; earth people—people just like you and me.

"How can I be so sure of that? Man alive, I look at applications for employment every single day of the week. I've interviewed thousands of people since I've been in personnel work. Sure, United Electric is tops in its field, but we've got just ordinary people working for us, too.

"How do we go about getting extraordinary results? *By getting each man and woman—every single employee in the plant—to do their level best.* That's how we do it, and that's how other top-notch outfits do it, too. Our policy is *always do your best.*

You can't do more, and you shouldn't want to do less. And even that's not original with us. A gentleman named General Robert E. Lee said that over a hundred years ago. It's still as true today as it was then."

Actually, Barney's stealing my thunder; he's getting into the second principle even before I can! So before he says any more, here it is:

2. The superiority of any organization depends upon the ability of its leader to bring the men of the lower group up to that level of skill and proficiency where they will become an asset to the entire organizational effort.

First, a bit of explanation is in order here, I think, so you can better understand this principle. You see, the men in the upper bracket (about 10 percent of your work force) are the best educated, the quickest to learn, and the easiest to motivate. *They must be challenged to develop their full potential.*

In the military, these men become the officers and the noncommissioned officers; in civilian life—they become the managers and the executives, the foremen and the supervisors.

The middle group must be stimulated to do their best.

The men in the middle group (about 80 percent of your work force) are the average run of American people. They are easily managed under normal circumstances. They take quite well to discipline and a certain amount of regimentation. They learn readily and respond well to competent and capable leadership. They cannot be bluffed or fooled by an incompetent leader for long.

Although alert and sharp, This group is also capable of doing far more than they try to do. Every man is as lazy as he dares to be and get by! *So this group must be stimulated to do their best.* Some people will tell you that this group has to be *pushed;* don't you believe it. They must be *pulled.* A leader cannot push from in front, and if he's a leader—that's where he has to be.

The lowest group requires your greatest motivational efforts.

In the lowest bracket (also about 10 percent of your work force) are those who need your attention most of all. You'll find that the disciplinary problems will always be higher here than in the average middle group or the top bracket. *The employees in this group need special motivation.* Their attitudes and their behavior act as a very special gauge which measures the lowest dip of the morale and esprit of your outfit.

Upon this group you must focus your attention and your greatest motivational efforts if you want to weld your unit into a superior one.

The military uses this principle, too.

"When I was at Fort Dix as a training company commander, we had a tremendous amount of competition between companies trying to get the highest score on the final eight week basic training proficiency test," says Major Mark Underwood.

"In the beginning, I made the mistake of concentrating most of my attention on the top men in the company—those who would normally be the A and B students in school. I thought if they could answer *all* the questions correctly, it would improve my overall score terrifically, but I was wrong. The trouble was, that group represented only a small part of my company; just about 10 percent—a percentage far too small to make any appreciable effect on the final company score.

"Then I focused my attention on the bottom part of the company—on those men who would be the lower C, D, and F students in school. My efforts here paid off, and I was deeply gratified to see the median score go up 8 points for my unit."

Use the system that pays off.

This, then, is the key in deciding which group of men most needs your personal attention. It's the lowest group, of course. Oh yes, there'll be some who won't respond; there always are, no matter how hard you try to help them. You'll have to get rid of them, and that's not an easy task, I know.

Today, with nearly every industrial plant in the nation unionized in some way, we've nearly gone beyond the point of saying, "Eliminate the inefficient employees; get rid of those who can't be assimilated!" It's hard to do; it's going to get a lot harder.

Oh, I know it would be so easy to say to your personnel manager, "You shouldn't have hired that person in the first place," but that makes about as much sense as the solution that's offered to the suffering alcoholic by the old-fashioned, out-of-date minister when he says, "You shouldn't have started drinking in the first place!" That kind of advice is just too late.

3. All your employees must want to do what you want them to do.

In supervising your employees, you can afford to take only one straight approach. You must make a certain basic assumption. *You must assume that your employees want to do what you want them to do.*

"I've found that when a large number of my employees do not respond to this basic assumption, the fault is usually mine," says Foster Wright, a foreman with Tidewater Oil. "So I immediately check my procedures, my instructions, and my subordinate supervisors to find out where the trouble lies.

"When one or two people are involved, especially if they're repeaters, I feel safe in assuming that they're at fault, and it's not me or my procedures that are to blame. Getting rid of them can be a long and tiring process sometimes, but for the benefit of all, both management and union, it has to be done. And you'll find that the union is just as anxious to get rid of worthless deadwood as you are! They have no desire to waste their money defending a lazy inefficient employee in a grievance case."

It's all a matter of their mental attitude.

Most people are pessimistic by nature; they expect the worst to happen. They're much like the old lady who prays for a sunny day as she leaves the house carrying an umbrella under her arm, and saying, "Oh well, it'll probably rain, anyway!"

Your employees are no different than you are when it comes to getting into the right mood to do something. To get yourself into the right frame of mind or the right mental attitude to tackle a difficult task requires a lot of courage—all you've got sometimes. You must have a high and sustained determination to complete what you want to accomplish, in spite of the adverse circumstances that may come up. And nothing really worthwhile has ever been accomplished without some obstacle being overcome. You must refuse to believe that there any any circumstances strong enough to defeat you in the accomplishment of your purpose.

Believe that it is so, and it will be so!

That's the kind of mental attitude you need, and it's the kind of attitude you need to infuse your employees with to get them to do what you want them to do.

In short, if you and your employees can adopt the slogan so many United States military units used during World War II and the Korean Conflict, you'll have it made. If you've ever been in service yourself, that slogan might be familiar to you, too. Remember it? "The hard things we do at once; the impossible takes a little time!"

Motivation is the real key to this principle.

Motivation is the key to using this third principle and making it work. That is, you'll have to know how to motivate each one of your employees to get him into the right frame of mind or the right mental attitude. Your motivational efforts will be different for each group of men, and actually, for each individual man. To use the right dynamic law of motivation on the right man at the right time, you must have a complete understanding of each one of your employees.

The motivation of men cannot possibly be covered in this short space. So in synopsis, I'd like to list some of the dynamic laws of motivation for you. They are—

1. *Know your men and look out for their welfare.*
 2. *Always keep your men informed.*
  3. *Make sure the task is understood, supervised, and accomplished.*
   4. *Train your men as a team.*
    5. *Develop a sense of responsibility in your subordinates.*
     6. *Motivate every single man to feel important to himself.*

As I said, the study of the motivation of others is a subject big enough to fill a book all by itself. In fact, it has, and if you'd like to learn the techniques to put these six dynamic laws of motivation—plus the other five for there are a total of eleven exact laws—into daily operation, then I'd suggest that you get a copy of *How to Use the Dynamics of Motivation* from Parker Publishing Company of West Nyack, New York.

It's chock-full of case histories and examples from top outfits such as Lily-Tulip Cup, McDonnell's, Kendall Refining, Sears Roebuck, J. C. Penney, General Motors, and many others. In fact, it's the best book on human relations and applied psychology to come down the pike in a long, long time.

To wrap this principle up.

For a quick wrap-up of motivation, or getting your employees to do what you want them to do, let me say this. The real art of motivation is to reach every man in such a way that each one will be stimulated to perform at his peak for you at all times. *That's real motivation.*

4. The superior outfit is the one who is better than any other in the field in ALL THINGS.

"Making an outfit a superior one takes the cooperation of every single employee," says Jack Miller. "I know, for I worked at several shipyards in World War II.

"When I came to the Albina Shipyard here in Portland, I stayed put. Everything about Albina was different; it was really an OK outfit."

Really, Jack is too modest, but perhaps he doesn't know the whole story. Here are some of the facts about the Albina Shipyard's, Oregon, record during World War II.

a. *It operated on its own money and refused government financing of its war orders.*

b. *Morale among Albina workers was so high that absenteeism was only 2.95 percent—the lowest in the United States.* (The industrial average at that time was eleven percent—nearly 4 times that of Albina!)

c. *Albina workers subscribed a total per man for war bonds that was nine times greater than the total per man in any other war plant.*

d. *Albina workers broke every subchaser building record.*

e. *Albina athletic teams won every war industries sport championship.*

f. *Albina's flag carried four Navy efficiency stars—the coveted Navy E for excellence—an honor given to no other American shipyard!*

g. *Because of Albina's outstanding record, the United States Government appointed it as an expediter for war materials for 35 other subchaser yards.*

Frank Knox, then Secretary of the Navy, was so impressed by Albina's record that he said, "Albina has done as much to improve the morale of the Navy as any other single influence since Pearl Harbor." (And the military services thought they won the war single-handed!)

Truly Albina's President, L. R. Hussa, knew how to build a superior outfit—with only ordinary people!

I've said there were four principles to follow in building a superior outfit with only ordinary average men, and that's true. But there's one other principle I've not mentioned. It's this:

No outfit can be 100 percent superior unless the boss is superior, too!

Unless you, as their leader, set the example for them to follow, they'll have no rallying point. You must be their standard bearer. Some leaders do it one way; others set an entirely opposite course. It all depends upon your own individual personality and your inherent capabilities as a leader.

For example, in Korea, one infantry division commander was a skilled banjo player. Up at the front, he formed a small band of enlisted men and fitted into it, not as the leader, but as the banjo player. Between fire fights and during the battle lulls, they played for the troops. The men loved him for it. Later, he went on to become one of the Army's ranking generals. His name was Arthur G. Trudeau, and he was quite a remarkable officer.

General Douglas MacArthur was also a superior leader, but I can't quite see him playing a banjo for his troops; can you? Maybe you can't play a banjo either. So each leader must follow his own natural instincts and develop his own talents to become a superior boss. However, there are five guidelines you can follow; here they are:

1. *You must have a strong belief in human rights.*
2. *You should have respect for the dignity of every person.*
3. *You must develop the Golden Rule attitude toward your daily associates.*
4. *You need to have an abiding interest in all aspects of human welfare.*
5. *You must have a willingness to deal with every man as if he were your blood relative.*

These qualities mark the man who is capable of pursuing a great purpose consistently in spite of heavy odds. He who has them will be looked upon as a man among men—a true leader of others. Pursue them with fidelity, with a steadfast faithfulness, and you will become the superior leader of a superior outfit.

The benefits of having a superior organization.

What are some of the benefits of using these basic principles to build a superior outfit? Well, I've just mentioned one benefit right there—*a superior outfit!*

Back in the beginning of this chapter, I told you some of the benefits, but since Albina is the classic example of superiority, let me review just four points of their record again; I think you can visualize the benefits yourself.

1. *Operated on its own money; refused government loans.* (That's not only a benefit and a sign of superiority; it's a miracle!)

2. *Morale was so high that absenteeism was only 2.95 percent.* (The national average in industry was eleven percent.)

3. *Individual purchases of war bonds were nine times greater than in any other war industries plant.*

4. *Albina earned four Navy E awards—an honor given to no other shipyard.*

Can you imagine the self-satisfaction of its president and his pride in his employees? Mr. Hussa had to be a remarkable man, for that's really a record to shoot for, my friend. I think it goes without saying that there'll be no limit to your profits if you can match that record. *So have at it!*

In conclusion, then . . .

Now that you know the principles of building a superior outfit with only average men, you need know only one more thing. *How to keep it on top once you've got it there.*

To keep it on top will take constant application of these principles, but further than that, it will take persistence. It will take a persistence that President Calvin Coolidge once described this way: "Nothing in the world can take the place of persistence. Talent will not; nothing is more common than unsuccessful men with talent. Genius will not; the world is full of educated derelicts. Persistence and determination alone are omnipotent. The slogan 'Press on!' has solved and always will solve the problems of the human race."

That's what it will take.

Use the Keen Edge of Competition — and Cut Your Way to Success

Desire is the first law of gain. And competition, or the effort to obtain something wanted by others, such as a position, a promotion, or a reward, springs from that deep desire for gain. However, competition covers a much broader scope than gain alone. Even a newborn child is in competition with its father, its brothers and sisters, for the attention of its mother. Unknowingly at first—later on, by definite design.

Competition can masquerade under many disguises. When it erupts as jealousy or envy or greed for another person's talents, possessions, or position, it becomes unhealthy and an undesirable motive force, just as it did when Cain and Abel brought their offerings to the Lord.

Or when David, king of ancient Israel, sent Uriah, the Hittite, into the forefront of the battle to be killed so that he might have his wife, Bathsheba. Competition for a woman, especially another man's wife, forms the eternal triangle that has been a boon to writers of fiction for as long as man has lived.

Or James and John when they asked to be shown a special preference over the rest of the twelve by being given seats on the right and left hand of Jesus in His kingdom.

However, competition, properly used, produces leaders. A man can have education and intelligence; he can have organizational ability; he might be able to make sound and timely decisions, but unless his drive is sparked by the enthusiasm of a competitive spirit, he is utterly worthless to you. Any business firm, company, or corporation, worthy of its name, always promotes competition to its employees.

What is a competitor?

For example, the other day while I was waiting to talk with the plant manager of Lily-Tulip Cup's Springfield, Missouri, branch, I noticed a small clipping on the employees' bulletin board. Its title was "What is a competitor?" and the author's name was Norton Spirit. The back side of this clipping was blank so I know it had not been taken from a magazine or a newspaper. I have no way of giving credit to the proper source except to mention the author's name, and that, I've already done.

I have never read a better description of what a competitor is and what he has to do to keep on competing. To me, it was a succinct summation of how better and better products are being continually developed in our highly competitive free enterprise system. I thought you'd enjoy reading it, too.

WHAT IS A COMPETITOR?

A COMPETITOR is a person who spends his days, and often his nights, dreaming up ways to give your customers better service. When he finds out how, it will be your turn to find still better ways to keep your customers happy.

A COMPETITOR sometimes does more for you than a friend. A friend is too polite to point out your weaknesses, but a competitor will take the trouble to advertise them.

A COMPETITOR is never too far away to affect jobs of your employees. If the quality of your work decreases, or the alertness of your service, he will prosper and everyone will feel the effect.

A COMPETITOR'S ability should never be underestimated. The business graveyard is full of companies who figured the competition was stupid, shortsighted, or just plain lazy.

A COMPETITOR helps make life worth living. He keeps you alert and in peak condition. Without his rivalry you would find the race less interesting and the victory less satisfying.

A COMPETITOR is hard to live with, but harder to live without. Competition brings progress by encouraging the development of better products at better prices. It makes the customer the boss of the economy.

—Norton Spirit

ARE YOU COMPETING?

Henry Ford II summed it up even more briefly. "Competition is the keen cutting edge of business," he said. "It's always shaving away at costs."

You can use that same sharp competition as a subtle supervisory tool to get the best from your employees. The desire to be on top—to be king of the hill—that in itself can keep many disciplinary problems from coming up simply by keeping your men's attention focused on a far different and much more exciting goal.

Later on, I'll give you specific examples of how two leaders used competition to bring out the best in their men. One was an army officer—a company commander in a basic training center; the other—a shift supervisor in a rubber plant.

In both cases, competition was used as a last ditch effort to weld a disorganized stubborn group of employees into a well-knit, hard-working, proud team. The results were amazing, not only to the two supervisors, but also, and just as important, to their superiors.

But first of all, before I get into the detailed techniques of how to get results in your supervision through competition, I'd like to show you some of the benefits you'll get when you do promote the spirit of friendly rivalry in your organization.

Here are a few of the good things you can expect to happen when you emphasize and promote competition.

1. *You'll increase the working output of every employee, from your janitor on up through the executive management level.*

2. You'll get increased production of a better quality product.

3. You'll develop your men's initiative and enthusiasm.

4. Competition always encourages the development of better products. It acts as a spur to your organizational growth and progress.

5. Competition will make your men keen and alert. Competition makes the job worthwhile; it makes life worth living.

6. When you get the results of 1 through 5—you'll make more money! You can't prevent it; you'll succeed in spite of yourself.

Throw down a challenge and get results.

"I consider my ability to arouse the competitive spirit in a man the greatest asset I have," says Earl Lane, a highly paid trouble-shooter at the executive level for the Dominion Corporation.

"When one of our plants, which manufactures plastic parts for the rest of our corporation, was having trouble meeting its production quota, I was sent down there to find out why. The plant manager could give me no answer; he couldn't lay his finger on the trouble. Nor could the production superintendent or his mill foreman. They all knew which department was at fault—but no one knew why.

"I was determined to find out for myself. I had to, for assembly lines in our other plants were bogged down for a lack of parts. We were in a critical position for some of our best customers, woolen and textile mills who use our parts in their big looms, were threatening to cancel their orders. I had to have a solution for the problem so I went right out on the production line to find my answer.

" 'How many units did your shift produce today?' I asked the shift supervisor.

" 'Three hundred,' was his answer.

"It was just about half his capacity. He knew it and so did I, but I said nothing more to him. Instead, I walked over to the mill department's bulletin board by the time clock. I tore a sheet of paper from my clipboard, tacked it up on the board and then wrote a big figure 3 on it. Then I simply turned my back on the supervisor and walked away.

"When the next shift came in, some of the men called the new supervisor's attention to the figure 3 on their bulletin board. Naturally, they wanted to know what it meant, and so did he. Not only was he told what it stood for, but he was also informed by the departing shift supervisor that it couldn't be topped! *The first supervisor was already rising to the bait!*

"How wrong that day shift supervisor was," Earl went on to say. "When he came back to work the next morning, he found the 3 had been crossed out and a new sheet of paper with a 5 on it was covering it up. *The second supervisor had also been hooked!*

"By the time I was ready to leave, that plant was exceeding its daily quota and was able to stockpile some of its production just in case a real emergency came along. Cost wise, it has risen from the least efficient plant in our system to the top one during the past year!"

What's the principle here?

You might now ask, "What's the principle here?" My answer is this: *You must throw down a challenge to get results.* When you do, you touch a man's competitive quick, and he'll rise to this stimulus when all else fails. It's a matter of pride. Earl Lane is paid a top salary for knowing how to inspire men to do their utmost. His method can be valuable to you, too.

What methods are used to promote competition?

There are four basic methods of competition based on this principle of throwing down a challenge to get results. These four basic methods are—
1. *Get a man to compete with himself—to beat his own record.*
  2. *Use competition between individuals.*
    3. *Use competition between groups or teams; departments or sections; branch stores or plants.*
      4. *Use competition with outsiders, with other companies or corporations.*

1. Get a man to compete with himself — to beat his own record.

Surfing, swimming, golf, running—even fishing—all these are competitive sports where one man's skills can be pitted against another man's, or *against his own previous record.* When you use this method in your plant or in your store, no man is in competition with another man; he's in conflict with his own errors.

Professionals use this system all the time.

"There's not a bowler living, and I don't care whether he's 7 or 70, who doesn't keep right on trying to roll that elusive perfect 300 game," says Dick Weber, member of bowling's Hall of Fame. "He's always trying to beat his last game, no matter how good it was."

And that's true in any sport. Every golfer goes for the hole-in-one every chance he gets. A pole vaulter sets a new world's record, and he goes right over the bar again—*trying to beat his own record!*

It's true in business, too.

Leaders in business and industry have the same competitive spark that leads to progress—to development of new methods and new ideas—to better and better products. Henry Ford's ambition was to build an ever increasing number of better cars at ever decreasing costs. That was his goal—to continually beat his own previous record. He was in competition with no one but himself. The corporation he founded, although in competition with others in many fields, still carries on his tradition in its slogan, "Ford has a better idea."

It works for the rank and file as well.

Wherever a record can be kept in black and white of previous efforts—this system of a man competing with himself can be used. Salesmen use it all the time. Every time he beats his past record, he makes more money for himself. Every life insurance salesman wants to become a member of the famed "Million Dollar Club." A line production worker can use the system and so can your secretary. It'll work for nearly everyone.

It's a stand-by at Lincoln Electric.

"The day is fast coming when the fixed hourly wage will be only a relic of the past in both business and industry," says Jim Goodwin, an executive with Lincoln Electric, one of the pioneers in the field of profit sharing. "The only employees who'll keep on working for a fixed hourly wage will be those employed in nonproductive, non-selling, service type jobs.

"Wage incentive and profit sharing plans have taught us a valuable lesson here at Lincoln Electric. Once you set a realistic quota based on a certain past standard of performance, your men will use every trick they can think of to beat the system so they can have a bigger take-home pay.

"And it's not only money that's at stake. You've challenged his ingenuity and his initiative when you set a standard. In effect, you're saying, 'This is the limit, the ceiling; you can't beat it.' But you just watch him; he will!"

Competition lets your supervisors concentrate on the job — not on the man.

If your employees have this kind of an interest in their work, your supervisors can concentrate on seeing that the real job is being done instead of having to play some silly cat-and-mouse game with a malcontent who can't pay his grocery bills and his rent on a straight hourly pay job. *The incentive system is the sneakiest kind of supervision you can use,* for it forces a man to be his own taskmaster.

2. Use competition between individuals.

Competition between individuals is also a valuable supervisory tool. Rivalry between two persons comes from the desire to win—the desire to excel. Competiton here is defined as an effort to gain something that is also wanted by others. It's a contest and that makes it worthwhile.

You've heard people say that it doesn't matter whether you win or lose, it's how you play the game that counts. Truthfully—I've never met anyone yet who cheered when he lost. Have you?

"It's all a matter of relativity, a matter of comparison," says Joe Wells, sales manager for Colgate Palmolive's Midwest territory. "It's a carry-over from childhood days and the idea of 'My dad can lick your dad.'

"Some of our salesmen go into a higher tax bracket when they go above their quotas; they keep only a fraction of their higher earnings. But each one wants to win—to beat the other salesmen. Each one wants to be the top salesman in the territory. That's the important thing to them."

Factories can use this system, too.

"One of the men on the black rock cutter—that's a machine that does most of the final shaping of V-belts—earns an average of 165 to 185 percent of his hourly base rate every day," says Warren Bentley, superintendent in charge of production for one of Dayco Corporation's subsidiary plants. "We don't have a man in his department who can come close to him in production, but *they always keep trying!*

"And that brings their own production up, too. More production means more money for all of us. And it keeps their attention where it ought to be—on their work. They don't have time to hatch up trouble for someone; they're too busy trying to beat the leader."

But what about the loser?

I've talked a lot so far in this chapter about the winner, and I'll have a lot more to say about him. But for now—let's take a second look at the loser.

This is especially important when you're dealing with the second method of competition—competition between individuals. It doesn't take a man long to spring back with enthusiasm when he fails to beat his own record. And when groups or teams or departments are competing—the losers can console each other. But here, it's important that you take some kind of action.

Keep in mind that the real purpose of competition is not to beat someone down in the dirt and trample on him, but to *bring out the best in every man.* So never demean the loser. Don't rub it in. He has lost, and that in itself should be enough. Bring him back into the fold by using the concept, "I will share with you the result of our common effort, even though I won." In short, *make sure the loser wins something, too!*

3. Use competition between groups or teams.

A while ago I mentioned two leaders who gained spectacular results when they used competition to bring out the best in their men. Both of them threw down a challenge to gain their results. First, let me tell you about the army officer, or better yet, let him tell you the story himself.

Soldiers go for competition.

"I was assigned as a basic training company commander at Fort Leonard Wood, Missouri," Major (then Captain) William Hale told me. "I was fresh from Vietnam, and the Battalion Commander, Colonel Cole, had given me command of B Company for it was his biggest headache. Discipline was miserable; morale and esprit were at rock-bottom. He hoped they'd listen to a combat officer. I was his last hope.

"Well, those men were mostly malcontents, nothing but troublemakers. They hated the army, were constantly in hot water. Now at the end of the eight-week basic training cycle, every man must pass a training proficiency test before he can go on to advanced training. If he fails, he must take at least part, sometimes all, of his basic training over again.

"It was the first time in Fort Leonard Wood's history that the Commanding General was thinking about keeping an entire company—over 200 men—for a second eight weeks of basic training!

"I was grasping for straws, willing to try anything. Even though I hadn't started out with this company, I knew how the army worked and how it thought, and I knew I'd end up as the goat simply because I was commanding it at the end. I could see my career going up in blue smoke. People back in the Pentagon just see the end results; they don't know all the circumstances.

"A couple of nights before the final eight-week test, I happened to read in the Infantry Journal about how another commander had the same kind of a problem and how he licked it. I thought, what have I got to lose? I'll try it.

"I waited until A Company took their test, for my B Company hated them. A Company made a tremendously good score of 91.4. The night before my B Company's test, my First Sergeant and I painted signs in bright red paint all over our company sidewalks and on the side of the barracks, like this: A Company—91.4; B Company—Zilch!

"The next morning at reveille I heard a lot of mumbling in the ranks. Questions flew back and forth. I heard my First Sergeant say, 'A Company must have visited us last night; couldn't have been anyone else. I guess they think B Company's worthless. What do you think, men?' The rumbling changed slowly to a roar of anger. B Company had been challenged; they rose to the task.

"They massacred the score of A Company. They not only broke that 91.4, but they rubbed it in. They broke the Battalion, the Regimental, and the Post records with a ringing 95.6! Their record still stands, too. How did they do it? Simple. *They'd been challenged!* They'd been slapped in the face and told they couldn't do it; so they did!"

And so does industry.

The other example I want to tell you about is that of a shift supervisor, Bob Richerson, in the industrial belt department of the Firestone Rubber Company. Bob had been assigned to the second shift, a stubborn hardheaded group, mainly because of his success in another department. Here though, he found himself faced with his biggest challenge.

The first afternoon Bob came to work in his new department, he found a mimeographed production sheet for the previous week's work on his desk. All three shifts were represented. Studying the figures, he saw that the second shift was lowest of all three in total incentive wages earned and in their total production. But it was highest in nonproductive hours and machine breakdown time.

"I'd planned on getting together with my shift, but I hadn't known quite what to say," Bob says. "This report seemed perfect for my purposes. At the end of the shift, I called the men around, and asked if their previous supervisor had ever discussed a production report with them. He hadn't. They'd never even heard of one—let alone seen one. And they were deeply interested in those figures.

"It didn't take them long to see what those figures meant in dollars and cents either. They simply hadn't known what the other two shifts were doing. And they'd never realized how much that lost production was costing them in take-home pay.

"That production sheet did my job for me. In one week the second shift was leading the department in total incentive wages earned and in total production. Nonproductive hours and machine breakdown time had become the lowest of all three shifts. All I did was *throw down a challenge* to them; they did the rest," Bob says.

And retailers, too.

"My store managers are in constant competition with each other," says Phil Newton, President of Newton Variety Stores, Incorporated, in Springfield, Missouri. "I have over a dozen stores scattered throughout the Springfield trade area. I even have one as far south as Branson, down on Lake Taneycomo.

"I've found that competition within my own system is one of the best ways to spur my managers to use their own initiative and ingenuity to boost sales. All of them work on a salary plus a percentage of the profits, but the top three in the system get a well-earned bonus at the end of the year. Their extra efforts earn them extra money, too. It's a good profitable method for everyone—even the losers!"

4. Use competition with outsiders, other companies and corporations.

There are times when competition between individuals and groups can be momentarily dropped to concentrate on the bigger goal—*competition with the real rival—the outsider.*

Two basic considerations must be used in applying this principle—

1. *Picking a proper opponent.*
2. *Determining the kind of competition.*

Pick the opponent.

It's not enough to say, "Let's lead our entire industry in sales this year." That's too vague, too nebulous, too indecisive. Wherever possible, *pick a real opponent, and pick only one opponent at a time.* Naturally, that opponent should be a competitive firm in the same line of business.

Let's take V-belts, for example.

The Springday Company, located in Springfield, Missouri, and a subsidiary of the Dayco Corporation, is at the present moment the world's largest producer of V-belts. What's a V-belt? It's the fan belt on your car; the rubber belt on your automatic dryer; the drive belt on your air-conditioner, your tape recorder, on practically any electric motor you can think of.

Now the Gates Rubber Company in Denver, Colorado, also makes V-belts, but not nearly as many. Springday is their natural opponent.

Grocery stores can profit by picking an opponent.

Here's the way one grocery store owner picked his opponent.

"I asked my wholesale suppliers how much they were selling to my biggest competitor two blocks down the street," says George Brown, who happens to be my own grocer. "Then I used their figures as quotas for my own store to shoot at.

"Truthfully, I think some of the figures they gave me were padded, but that didn't hurt me a bit. It helped, in fact. I had those figures posted on a board in the back of my store. If my competitor bought 20 cases of a certain item each week, then it was safe to assume he was selling that many.

"My employees started pushing the items I had set quotas on—suggesting them to every customer—and we've been moving about 10 percent more merchandise in those lines ever since."

The government can give you figures.

If you can't get accurate figures about your own competition locally, you can get some ideas from the Bureau of the Census, United States Department of Commerce, Washington, D.C. Write to them for copies of the *Annual* Census of Manufactures or the *Monthly* Retail Trade Report. From these you can get progress figures for your line of business. Some are broken down geographically by areas. Against these you can rate your own company's performance.

Look back at those V-belts, for instance. If the figures are given for the midwest, and there are only two of you, and you know your own production figures—well?

Determine the kind of competition.

Your competition can be in total number of sales, dollar and cent wise. If this makes your non-salespeople—the production employees, shipping clerks, office workers, etc., feel left out—you can run your competition in terms of total profit figures. Everyone's involved in that.

Or you could run several contests all at the same time. Your production versus another company's production—with the proper handicap to one of you, just as in bowling. Use sales versus sales; total profit against total profit. You can bet the big car manufacturers do this, and so do companies like Coca-Cola, 7-Up, and Pepsi-Cola. Sure it takes some imagination, some ingenuity, and some effort to do all this. *Competition never is easy; it's a challenge to you!*

Your guidelines to control competition.

As a leader, there are a few guidelines that you should follow to properly control the four methods of competition that you're supervising. They are—

1. Stimulate your men by competition — don't irritate them.

Highly competitive periods have to be followed by breathers, or everyone will go sour. Run your competition with high and low pressure areas. It takes valleys to make the peaks.

2. Keep track of what's happening.

Don't allow competition to run wild to the point that anything goes. You must maintain control.

3. Keep an impartial attitude.

Don't take sides. Any competition must be open and above board to be useful. Don't play favorites or get involved. As management—you can't afford to win.

4. Keep people informed.

Let everyone know what's going on and who's ahead. If you use progress charts, keep them up to date. If you can't do that—throw them away. They're nothing but eyewash.

Memory Markers.

Let's review now and see if these benefits of promoting competition aren't better than using a big club to supervise your employees. Remember, if you emphasize and promote competition, you'll get six specific results.

1. *You'll increase the working output of every employee.*
2. *You'll get increased production of a better quality product.*
3. *You'll develop your men's initiative and enthusiasm.*
4. *Competition always encourages the development of better products. It acts as a spur to progress and growth.*
5. *Competition will make your men keen and alert. Competition makes the job worthwhile: it makes life worth living.*
6. *When you get these results (1 through 5) you'll make more money. You can't prevent it; you'll succeed in spite of yourself.*

And to get these specific benefits, here's all you have to do . . .

1. *Get a man to compete with himself—to beat his own record.*
  2. *Use competition between individuals.*
    3. *Use competition between groups or teams; departments or sections; branch stores or plants.*
    4. *Use competition with outsiders, with other companies or corporations.*

How to Use the Five High C's of Control

Man has learned to control fantastic machines that can crawl or creep, run or fly; he's learned how to tunnel through the earth and how to orbit it. With one kind of machine he can search the ocean depths; with another he can land on the moon. He's learned how to harness energy and how to control its expenditure at will. But only a rare few have learned how to properly control another human being's actions.

Of course, I'm not concerned here with controlling others by the use of force or threats, fear or starvation. I'm not talking about slavery or human bondage or the kind of control exercised by dictators like Genghis Khan or the Nazis and the Japanese in World War II. Nor do I have in mind the kind of control the Communists use.

Nor can you control a man by logic alone.

An IBM machine, a computer, any piece of machinery can be controlled by the use of experience, intelligence, logic, and reason—but not a man. Why? Because a machine has no emotions. A machine cannot cry or get angry or fall in love or wear a miniskirt or a bikini.

Why is it that a tabloid newspaper will outsell a clean, well-edited, conservative paper by ten-to-one? Because it appeals to the emotions, that's why!

Even today a fire-and-brimstone revival preacher can fill a huge amphitheater (many carry their own air-conditioned tents now on huge tractor and trailer combinations) while your own minister preaches to a church that is less than half-filled. Why? Because your minister wants you to think that he's a sensible, normal, rational individual; so he appeals to your logic, your reason, and your common sense. But the revival preacher appeals to your emotions!

When Mohammed first preached his doctrines, they were sane and sensible and moderate; he attracted but few converts. When he added emotion—his new religion swept over half the known world!

Oh yes, appeal to a man's logic and reason by all means. Give him a rational motive for doing what you want him to do. But if you really want to stir him to enthusiastic action, base your request upon one of his primary emotions—love, gain, duty, pride, self-indulgence, and self-preservation.

It's all a matter of control.

You see, controlling people boils down to appealing to their emotions to *get them to do what you want them to do.* And getting them to do what you want them to do is a definite and concrete benefit you'll gain when you learn how to properly control your employees. They'll want to do what you want them to do *if they get what they want* while they're doing it. But you must remain in control at all times, never let them get into the driver's seat.

For instance, when you control your car, it goes where you want it to go; when it's out of control—it goes where it wants to go! I'm reminded of the highway sign I saw while driving through Alabama a few years ago. "When you drive faster than 70—you're not controlling your car—you're aiming it!"

And people out of control are worse than a car. They can think and plan and scheme; a car can't.

Here's another big benefit you'll gain from proper control.

When you can achieve this first benefit of getting people to want to do what you want them to do, and making sure that they get what they want while they do it, you'll automatically gain another big benefit, and it's this:

You'll have employees who will respect you and have confidence in you, who will give you their willing obedience, their loyal cooperation, and their full support.

And that, my friend, is real control of people.

The Five High C's of Control.

Control depends upon communication, coordination, cooperation, correlation, and correction. These are the Five High C's of Control.

And that's what I'm going to cover in the rest of this chapter: how to supervise your employees by using those Five High C's of Control—
  1. *Communication,*
   2. *Coordination,*
    3. *Cooperation,*
     4. *Correlation,*
      5. *Correction,*

and then start from the top all over again.

Your control of people is a five step process

First of all, you must *communicate your desires* to your men. You must let them know what you want them to do. Next, you must *coordinate their activities* toward a common goal. Third, you must *cooperate with them,* and have them cooperate with each other to insure the achievement of that common goal. Fourth—you should *correlate the results and the findings* with your original desires so you can *correct the mistakes*—the fifth step.

Then you start all over again and *communicate your new desires* based on the results of your findings. And that, in general, is how to control your employees with the Five High C's. Now for the specifics:

1. The First High C of Control — Communication.

The degree to which you, as a supervisor, a manager, an executive, or whatever your capacity happens to be as a leader, can make your policies and your decisions known, understood, and accepted by your employees will materially influence your own effectiveness on the job.

Unless your people know and understand what you want them to do, they'll never do it. Their acceptance of you depends upon the methods you use to transmit your orders or your requests, i.e., whether you use an authoritarian or a democratic manner in your approach.

Communication is one of the most difficult and most important aspects of your supervisory responsibility. And the higher you go in the chain of command in management, the more difficult communication with your employees will become.

Your communication, to be effective and worthwhile, must not only convey information, but it must also motivate the man on the receiving end to want to receive and to understand what you're trying to tell him. Just talking is not necessarily communication. Remember this before you ever issue a single order or post a directive on the company bulletin board.

Your employee must want to carry out your order; he must see how it benefits him. And he'll never want to carry it out unless he is benefited by doing so. Your order must help him get what he wants.

Your control of people is based on their desires — not yours.

Top salesmen like Elmer Wheeler or Frank Bettger have learned well the secret of controlling another person's behavior so it will benefit them. So have the leaders in any field, no matter what it is. However, the secret of this control of others is a little more visible or more readily understandable in the field of salesmanship.

What is that secret? *Desire—or what the other fellow wants.* If you can find out what another man wants specifically and then *help him get it*—he'll do whatever you want him to do, just as long as he gets what he wants while he's doing it.

Why most people miss.

The trouble with most people is twofold. They might find out what another man wants, but they forget all about the second half—helping him get it. Why? Well, usually because they're too interested in themselves—and not the other fellow. They go on to tell him how important their own desires are, and naturally, the other fellow couldn't care less. He's concerned about what he wants—not what you want.

Now there's not a thing wrong with telling another man how much you need him—how much you need his help—how you can't possibly get along without him. That's wonderful—you're appealing to his ego—to his pride. You're making him feel important by telling him that you need him; *and that's one of his primary desires—to feel important!*

I personally have used this approach for nearly 30 years with everyone I've ever had any dealing with at all, and it's never failed me yet. "I need your help!" is one of the most potent sentences you can use. I know many a salesman who has closed an otherwise impossible sale with those words.

You see, most people are a lot like automobiles. They can be pushed or pulled along, or they can be stirred into action by igniting their own motive power. But it's up to you to provide the proper fuel. The only kind of fuel that will start the action you really want inside that person is appealing to one of his basic desires. That's the only way you'll ever control a man and be able to get what you want from him at the same time.

The hidden secret.

This is the secret secret! It's the deep hidden part of the secret that should never come to light. That is—whenever he gets what he wants by doing what you want him to do—*you will get what you want, too!* That fact should never be openly apparent to him. If he does happen to see it, it should not appear to be important to you at all. It should seem to be just coincidental, or better yet—make it seem as if you'd get rid of it if you could.

Suppose you're a salesman, for example. A salesman shows his prospect how he can make more money by buying his product. Now you show me someone who isn't interested in making more money! Of course, when the prospect is converted into a full-fledged customer, the salesman makes more money, too, but that fact is never brought out into the light for the buyer to see at all. It's kept better hidden than an old maid's girdle.

Industrial leaders use this secret.

If they didn't, they wouldn't be industrial leaders. Listen to how Al Denning, a plant manager for Allied Radio and Television, puts it:

"All our employees in the plant work on an incentive basis," Al says. "So the more they produce in a day, the more money they make. Time and time again, I've stopped by a fellow's machine, and after I've looked all around to make sure that no one else is listening—I make a great to-do about this, for I want to look extremely confidential;

you know how everyone wants to be let in on the big secret—I whisper to him something like this:

" 'Why don't you twist it this way each time, Fred? You'll gain at least three seconds every time you do.'

"Is he going to make more money? Of course he is. Isn't that what he wants? You know it is. Will I make more money, too? Yes, I will, for I work on a salary plus a percentage of the production. The more he produces, the more money the corporation makes, and the more money I make. Does he know that? No, not really, and even if he did, he'd never stop to really think about it; he's interested only in himself!"

Difficult or not — it's a must.

Without effective communication, there can be no coordination, no cooperation, no correlation, no correction of your end results. When these steps are missing, you have no control whatever of your employees. If the necessary information is missing on which to base the rest of your activities, you can't function. So your first step is to *communicate*.

You can't control from isolation.

"Whenever a person is promoted to a higher management level, he must make sure he doesn't become an office isolationist," says Leon Horner, a junior vice-president with the National Biscuit Company. "When I first became the junior VP in charge of production, I think I was overly impressed with my title and my name on the door in gold letters. I temporarily forgot all the principles of personnel management and the fundamentals of human relationship that I'd learned on my way up. I thought a big mahogany desk and a thick rug were more important than people.

"So I developed a cold impersonal—even haughty—attitude toward the men I'd formerly rubbed elbows with, and we lost complete contact with each other. I simply wasn't able to communicate my desires to them; without communication, there's no cooperation and no coordination at all. I wasn't getting the job done for I'd completely lost control of my people.

"To control your employees, you must communicate your desires to them, and you sure can't do that if you're isolated from them in your office. You've got to reach out to your people and get your ideas across if you want to maintain control of them. You must communicate. Fail to do that, and you're dead!"

Let your subordinates get into the act, too.

"It's my responsibility to keep my people informed so they'll know what's going on," says Harold Clausen, a department manager with International Harvester. "When I first took over this department, I wasn't specific enough when I issued my orders. I knew what I wanted, but I couldn't seem to use the right words to get my men to visualize my ideas. So things never turned out the way I expected them to. The place was full of surprises all day long.

"Once I learned to bring my supervisors into my confidence, things went along a lot better. Now I give them every opportunity I can to participate in the development of departmental plans, policies, and procedures. Through this participation, they have a much better understanding of the problem and the reasons behind my decision. As Jimmy Durante always says, 'Everybody wants to get into the act!' So I let 'em."

Communication is a two-way street, not just a one-way affair. Information has to pass both ways before you can ever get coordination and cooperation. Having your subordinates participate in your planning is one of the best ways to insure good communication.

Communicate progress — as well as orders.

One of the best ways to motivate your men to do their best for you is to keep them well-informed about the progress that they're making. Everyone wants to know how well he has done. And he also wants to know exactly what you expect from him. If you keep your people informed about their individual progress on the job—if you'll let them know where they stand with you—you'll encourage their initiative and enthusiasm, their teamwork and their morale.

So whenever you can, let your employees know how things are going. Keep them up to date. Post results where everyone can see where he and his outfit stands. You can use company bulletin boards or mimeographed handouts.

Watch your language though, or you're liable to come up with one like this classic out of World War II which read, "Men with complaints will be made in the Company Orderly Room today."

2. The Second High C of Control — Coordination.

Coordination means to bring scattered and separate elements or activities into a common action, movement, or condition. Cooperation means the act of working together toward a common goal in a united effort. We usually think of employees cooperating with each other or working together in a department while the activities of all the departments are coordinated. This immediately implies that cooperation can be accomplished without higher supervision, but that coordination requires the supervision of some higher authority.

Although the two terms are not completely interchangeable, they are most definitely compatible with each other. Coordination is required before cooperation can be fully obtained, but they go hand in hand like bacon and eggs.

Coordination usually means timing.

In common everyday usage, coordination most often means timing. A coordinated attack at Oh-five-hundred would mean to a military man that at 5 a.m., the infantry, the artillery, the armor, etc., would all combine their efforts at that precise time to blast the enemy out of existence.

So coordination, then, more than anything else, means the *proper timing of some action*. Timing is all important to a batter, a quarterback, a bowler, a swimmer, even a stock car racer. It's a must in any sport to any athlete. "He's a well-coordinated player" is a common phrase in sports. And it's a must in business, too.

Success in business often depends upon proper timing.

I asked Roger Ward, a technical representative with Le Tourneau, manufacturer of those huge earth-moving giants, if he felt that timing was important in their business. Here's what he has to say about it.

"In our kind of work, it's one of the biggest factors," Roger says. "It's a matter of being at the right place at the right time, simple and old-fashioned as that may sound.

"Just take the construction business, for example, where almost all of our equipment is used. There, contracts are let with a penalty clause if the specified completion date is missed. A successful contractor is an expert in many fields, but most of all *he's an expert in timing; in coordinating* the flow of the materials required to get to the job at the proper time in the right amounts, with exact specifications, with proper qualities, so that nothing is overlooked, work is not delayed, and nothing arrives too early or too late in too much or too little. That's the secret of a successful contracting business: *Timing—coordination.*"

Even the proper use of time is timing.

You'll hear all sorts of lectures and talks; you'll read all kinds of articles and books about how to save time. I ask you now—who can save time? No one. You can't put it in the bank or stuff it in a mattress or a tin can like money.

You'll even have efficiency experts tell you how to make the proper use of time in their time and motion studies in your plant. But remember this, too, about an efficiency expert. He's only the fellow who's called in to share the blame when things go wrong!

The important point for you to remember about time is this: *The proper use of time is timing, and timing is coordination.*

3. The Third High C of Control — Cooperation.

What's the best way to insure cooperation from your subordinates? Spell it with just two letters—*WE!* All joking aside, though, here's one of the best ways. Don't limit your information to just specific orders and directives when you're communicating your desires to your employees. *Always include some background data and some related and pertinent information.* Satisfy the fellow's natural curiosity. Tell him why the job has to be done that way and why it's important to you that it is.

Say it with flowers.

Many of the things you have to talk about and write about in your business might not have any real human interest—or so you think at first glance. There's nothing really very exciting to the average man about reading a production report or a sales report unless you touch it up a bit. Give the man who's reading it a real reason to *want* to read it. Something like this—

"Production exceeded our quota last month because the third shift in the sleeve department topped their standard by 24 percent. Jack Knox, the supervisor in charge, is to be congratulated!"

You think your people won't read it with interest now? They'll even read between the lines about what the first and second shifts didn't do, too; you don't have to say a thing about them. It's there, anyway!

So put a little spice into it; that's the fiction of nonfiction. Embellish your orders and your directives a bit; say it with flowers. As Rudolf Flesch would say, "Use the grammar of gossip!"

Cooperation is a principle of leadership.

If you will apply this principle of leadership, you can develop the desire on the part of your subordinates to cooperate and exchange vital information throughout your entire organization, especially up and down your command management lines.

If your subordinates are not cooperating with you in reporting information promptly and properly, without a doubt they're afraid of being criticized or punished. By the same token, this same fear of criticism or punishment will often cause a lack of desire in your subordinates to take the required corrective action, or it will be the underlying reason for their failure to meet your specified objectives. You cannot gain cooperation through the use of threats or fear.

If you gain the confidence, the respect, and the loyal cooperation of your subordinates, you'll have no trouble at all in communicating with them. But you can't communicate unless you cooperate. So do it!

4. The Fourth High C of Control — Correlation.

Now it's time to start checking on the results of the first three High C's of Control. This leads you to the Fourth High C—*Correlation.* This is the phase where you *start checking the results of your orders against the desires* contained in those orders.

If you haven't got what you actually wanted, it's now time to find out why. *What* actually happened? *Who* was at fault? *Where* did things go wrong? *When* did it happen? *How* can I correct it now? You must check, recheck, and then check some more, so you'll know what action to take.

The phase of critical analysis.

"I look at correlation as the phase of critical analysis," says Henry Myers, a supervisor with Boeing Aircraft. "There's absolutely no room for error in our specifications for building an airplane. It can't be almost, or not quite, or just about. With us—it's got to be just right! Mistakes in our business pay off in death for someone. And I sure don't want to feel that I'm responsible for someone being killed, so we've got to correct our mistakes before they get out of the factory."

Don't do it alone.

You can't do this step all by yourself. It takes full cooperation from all your employees, especially your subordinate supervisors. They should be able to help you correctly analyze, properly evaluate, and recommend sound courses of action on the problems they've found—the variance between your expressed desires and the final results. When you've finished with this phase of correlation—you're ready to move into the final High C of Control—Correction.

5. The Fifth High C of Control — Correction.

Do you know what to do now? Fine; do it! Once you've reached this point—don't hesitate. Too many supervisors are afraid to make a move here for they don't like to admit they were at fault, and any corrective action is, of course, an immediate admission of error!

But you must take the corrective action that's required, no matter who's at fault, even if it's your boss. To fail to do so is about like throwing more money in the pot when you know you've got a losing poker hand. You wouldn't call another man's bet if he's got three of a kind staring you in the face when you've got a single pair. There's just no sense in throwing good money after bad!

It's better to lose just a little face.

"Sure, it's hard to admit that a mistake's been made," says Julius Moore, a chemical engineer with Loring Chemical Company. "In our business, we can always palm it off as an experiment instead of a mistake. But it's still a mistake, and although we might fool some people, we can't kid ourselves here in the lab. I know that no one likes to lose face, as the Oriental says, but it's better to lose just a little face than to end up with no face at all."

Corrective action is a sign of moral courage.

Remember this about corrective action; it's a sign of your moral courage. So put the solution you've chosen into effect. Use techniques and methods that fit you—that are appropriate to your individual personality.

And don't be satisfied with merely initiating the corrective action. Don't be satisfied with surface appearances. Success will usually depend upon your ability and your willingness to supervise and check the results of your corrective action. So don't be satisfied; satisfaction brings only complacency and stagnation. *Unsatisfaction brings success.*

Generals aren't paid to be satisfied.

"I thought I was going to be cashiered out of the service by the Commanding General at Ford Ord," says Lieutenant Colonel Grant Mosher. "And it all had to do with my being satisfied with surface appearances—but the General wasn't!

"I was the Officer of the Day, and General C. S. Lyons had just finished inspecting the guard and the guardhouse for which I was responsible. 'Captain, I'm not happy with the appearance of your guard or the condition of your guardhouse,' he said to me. 'The men are sloppy and unshaven and the building looks like a trash dump. No, I'm not at all satisfied with your performance of duty on this.'

" 'General, I'm sure you're not,' I said. 'After all, *Generals aren't paid to be satisfied!*'

"His gray mustache bristled; his stone cold eyes glared at me and then he growled, 'You'd better explain that, Captain!'

"I was sweating blood by then, but I said, 'General, if you're satisfied, everything will go to pot in a hurry; as long as you're not satisfied, people will keep on their toes for you!'

"I waited for the explosion, but it never came. Instead he smiled—not much, but just a little bit—and said, 'I believe you're right, Captain. *Generals definitely aren't paid to be satisfied.* It is my job to keep this post in tiptop shape, and to keep people on their toes. So you'd better start stretching, young man, for I'm sure not satisfied with you!' "

Check points.

Do you see now how you can benefit by using the Five High C's of Control in your organization? Can you visualize how you can control people and get them to do what you want them to do? Do you understand how these Five High C's of Control will give you employees who'll respect you and have confidence in you, employees who will give you their willing obedience, their loyal cooperation, and their full support?

If you can, then put these Five High C's of Control to work for you. Remember them. They're—

1. *Communication,*

2. *Coordination,*
   3. *Cooperation,*
      4. *Correlation,*
         5. *Correction.*

Use these Five High C's of Control properly and your people will always be up to date all the time on new developments. They'll know well in advance whenever changes are coming. And as members of your team, they're entitled to know what's going on, and why and when.

So give them information about your company and the industry itself. Let them see themselves and their work in the proper perspective. They're entitled to benefits from the Five High Cs of Control, too.

How to Get Your Men to Go for Broke!

Want to win the victory in spite of seemingly impossible odds against you? *Then appeal to a man's emotions; establish an emotional rallying point!*

Want to see your men push you and your company to the top of the heap? *Give them a goal to shoot for!*

Want every man in your outfit to be his own self-starter? *Give him a blueprint for action!*

Want to get your men up and out of the rut of boredom? *Make their goal exciting and worthwhile!*

Want to keep his enthusiasm burning at fever-pitch? *Cheer him on from the sidelines!*

Want to get your men to *GO FOR BROKE? Give them a cause to fight for!*

They gave it their all.

World War II gave birth to the famous Japanese-American Regiment, the 442nd, better known as the *Go for Broke* outfit. "Go for Broke" is the pidgin English translation for their regimental motto of *give it your all.* And the 442nd did just that. They gave it their all; they went for broke! One battalion of the 442nd became known as the *Purple Heart Battalion* because of its high number of casualties. It was one of the most decorated outfits in World War II.

Once in Italy Ernie Pyle asked Kamejiro Matsumoto, "Lieutenant, why did you push on to capture that town the way you did? You knew the odds were all stacked against you."

Kamejiro answered in words that were to become immortal, not only in the 442nd, but also in the entire United States Army. "We had to," he said. "We fight double. One war against the Germans; the other war for every Japanese in America." And as Pyle reported, "They're winning both wars!"

And so did he . . .

It's one thing to fight on against seemingly impossible odds when you're part of a group or a member of a team. It's quite another when you're one man alone in a laboratory. It's so easy to become discouraged when you're only one individual fighting it out by yourself. Solitude can so often lead to self-pity. But it didn't in the case of Joseph Pirone.

Joseph is president of an internationally known cosmetics firm that counts its annual net receipts in several millions of dollars, but it wasn't always that way. In fact, less than 25 years ago, Joseph was fresh out of college with his sheepskin to certify that he had a degree in chemistry, and full of fire to lick the world. He had no idea of the odds against him. And it's best that he didn't. Even when warned by wholesale drug and cosmetic supply houses that he was tackling an impossible job that even better men than he had failed at, he nevertheless set out to do the job.

"It took every cent I could spare from my job as a junior chemist with a petroleum refining company to buy laboratory equipment, chemicals, and ingredients for my cosmetics experiments," Joseph says. "I'd mix a formula, and I'd put half in the refrigerator and half in the kitchen window in direct sunlight. I wanted a foolproof formula that would stand up in any kind of household temperatures and any type of treatment.

"Well, nearly two years of hard work went by. One morning, somewhere in the twenty-third month, I set my six hundred and seventy-ninth experiment out—one part in the refrigerator, the other part in the kitchen window. As I did, the thought came to me: The prevention of mold and deterioration is not from some substance outside the cosmetic; *the prevention of mold is within the mold itself,* and therefore—*inside the ingredients of the cosmetic!*

"From then on, it was a downhill slide. I don't know how many more experiments I made, but it didn't matter. I had the answer. From that moment, it was almost like picking up the parts of a picture-puzzle that have spilled out on the floor."

Joseph Pirone makes it sound so simple when he tells it today, but he had the courage to keep on trying after failing hundreds of times. He really knows what it means to *go for broke!*

And what about Thomas Edison? I have no idea of how many experiments he conducted before he came up with his first incandescent lamp, but his records show that by the twenty-first day of October in 1879, the day of his first successful attempt, he had spent *more than forty thousand dollars* in fruitless experiments! Think of how many dollars that sum would represent today. But he never gave up. He, too, knew how to *go for broke!*

All right, you've seen how one outfit and a couple of men did it. Now let's get into some of the techniques and see how you can do it, too.

1. Establish an emotional rallying point.

To inspire your people and to unite them solidly behind you, give them an emotional rallying point. Facts and figures are terrific, perhaps, for nearsighted bookkeepers, statisticians, and slide rule experts, but you'll never get a man to go all out for you by simply quoting a mass of indigestible facts and figures to him. You've got to appeal to one or more of those six basic prime movers of his:

1. *Love,*
2. *Gain,*
3. *Duty,*
4. *Pride,*
5. *Self-indulgence,*
6. *Self-preservation.*

Appeal to his heart — not his head!

You can give a man all sorts of logical reasons why a certain task should be done, but you're only appealing to his intellect. You've got to make your appeal to his emotional instincts. And the more motives you can appeal to, of course, the more successful you will be. Your success will depend greatly upon your own insight and your own powers of persuasion.

Politicians do it, too!

"That's why politicians pour their emotions into their statistics," says Jack Whaley, a former congressman from Nebraska. "Your senator could tell you quietly and calmly how much money he's saved you in taxes and how that new military base that's bringing so much money into your city would never have been approved by the Pentagon without his congressional influence, but he won't stop there. No sir!

"He'll wave his arms; he'll pound the table to make his point dramatic. He'll shake hands, kiss babies, and pass out cigars to his constituents. And he'll pat you on the back and tell you that you're the backbone of America; you're her courage and her strength. Why? Well, he knows the score about human nature, too, so he's making his pitch to your emotions—not to your intellect!"

Appeal to a man's daydreams.

And Jack's right, too. The average man, no matter what his social or economic status happens to be, sees himself in his daydreams as a lover, a fighter, a champion of human rights, God's gift to the world. In my day the idols were Tarzan (still a pretty durable figure), the Lone Ranger, Buck Rogers, Babe Ruth, and Tom Mix.

And then along came Batman, Mission Impossible, Matt Dillon, and Mickey Mantle. Every generation has a set of heroes; every man has his own daydreams. Don't break his bubble of happiness by telling him it just isn't so. If you want to get him on your side, appeal to one of those six basic emotions of his to get him shifted into overdrive.

Meet a master of the art.

General Douglas MacArthur, who graduated number one in his West Point class of 1903, was considered by most of his fellow officers to be a human IBM machine; in truth, he was the most brilliant military tactician this country has ever seen. He will also be remembered by many others as a most able administrator during his five years as the Supreme Commander of occupied Japan.

Still others will never forget his daring, his initiative, and his ingenuity in making the Inchon landings in Korea, a maneuver that broke the back of the North Korean Army and put them in complete rout back to the banks of the Yalu River.

But brilliant as he was, General MacArthur also knew that he had to appeal to the sentiments of the average man—the ordinary GI. That's why the symbols of a corncob pipe and a battered cap with its gold embroidered visor turning green from crusted sea salt linger in the memories of those who knew him. His words, "I shall return," served as an emotional rallying point for Americans when they were in the depths of despair as the heroic forces on Bataan and Corregidor were forced to surrender to the Japanese.

And when he was relieved from command in Korea in April, 1951, he could have slipped completely from the memory of the country had he turned bitter and vindictive. But he held this country in the hollow of his hand with his speech to Congress, especially with his closing words, "Old soldiers never die; they just fade away."

General MacArthur was a master of the art of appealing to a man's basic emotions.

Pearl Harbor was the emotional rallying point of World War II.

There never has been (at least, to my knowledge) a popular war. If there ever was one, I think World War II would have come close to being it. Why? *Because the American people had been given an emotional rallying point—and that, by the enemy!*

When the Japanese attacked Hawaii on the seventh of December, 1941, their victory was in reality their first defeat. Although a highly successful military maneuver from the Japanese point of view, for their attack crippled our powerful Pacific fleet, it was the first of a series of their mistakes in underestimating the will of the American people to fight. *Pearl Harbor served as the emotional rallying point for the United States in World War II.*

2. Give your men a goal to shoot for.

"Your men should know where they're going, what they're doing, and why they're doing it so they can plan their time intelligently and do their work effectively," says Frank Crane, a plant foreman with General Foods. "Good employees do not enjoy just working from day to day. You must take active steps to make clear to them the relationship between their daily work and the *big picture*—the larger company objectives."

How not to do it.

So many times I've heard foremen and supervisors, executives and managers, say to a man who's missed his chance for promotion, "You failed because you didn't have a goal to shoot for. You can't possibly succeed unless you know where you're headed!"

True, I agree with what they've said so far. But they never say enough! What happens next? Well, the average person who has failed is anxious to succeed. He wants to know where he's made his mistake, so he says, "I'd sure like to get ahead—but I don't know how! Please tell me what to do."

What's the average answer he gets? Listen for yourself. "Well, of course, you've got to consider all the factors bearing on your case. Each person is different so the situation is never quite the same. But you've got to set goals for yourself; can't just drift, you know. That's why you didn't get promoted this time. Excuse me, I'm late for my two o'clock meeting. Maybe we can get a chance to discuss your particular situation later on." And does he ever do that? You know the answer, too, don't you?

That, I don't agree with!

Nor do I go along with such vague generalities as "wealthy by middle age" or "retire sometime before you're 65" or "you might be promoted to foreman some day." *When?* That's the big question, isn't it? When is all this going to happen? You must know exactly where you want to go and when you want to get there before you can ever start to arrive. In short, be specific with your people. And you can do it if you—

3. Give them a blueprint for action!

You'll be surprised at how quickly a definite plan written down in black and white can change a man's attitude and approach from wandering vague generalities to exact and meaningful specifics. You can help him break up his plan into an outline form with intermediate steps that can be checked off frequently to show signs of his progress. Let a man keep his own individual progress chart and it'll help to keep him in high gear.

Help a man to formulate his own goals.

Maybe one man's goal is to make more money on the same job. Then show him what he has to do to reach that goal. Perhaps another employee is interested in getting a new job in your company. Tell him what he'll have to learn and be capable of doing before he can be transferred. Help your people to reach their goals and you won't have to push them any longer to get them going. *They'll be their own self-starters.*

A man's goal should be simple.

"It should have but one object; keep him on course; make him cheerful and enthusiastic about his work; be exciting and interesting," says Walter Stark of Kaiser Industries. "Make a man's goal too complicated—give him too many objectives to shoot for all at the same time and you'll defeat your whole purpose.

"One goal at a time is enough. Don't confuse him. You'll never keep him cheerful and enthusiastic by sending him off in a dozen different directions all at the same time. A baby fox, when first jumping a covey of quail, will try to catch four or five birds. He gets none. He'll not make that same mistake again. From then on, it's one at a time for him. Unfortunately, most of us aren't as smart as a fox; at least—in some things!"

What is success?

If you'll help a man by giving him a blueprint for action, you'll be helping him to become successful—to get what he wants out of life. And that's what success really is, isn't it? *Getting what you want from life!*

To help him, and just to make sure there is some overlapping and no stopping short of his final goal, never let him check off an intermediate step as finished until he's started to work on the next one.

You see, a successful individual doesn't grab for the top rung of the ladder on his first attempt. He sets each new goal just a little bit above his last achievement. These individual new goals are those intermediate steps he uses to attain his final ideal. But his real goal for his next step is only a few inches above his last one. And even as the crippled fellow, who climbs the stairs by going up two steps and slipping back one each time, eventually reaches the top—so will he.

Point a man in the right direction.

A young foreman I knew at Du Pont was in charge of one of their smaller departments. It was evident that he'd gone as far up the ladder as he could go without further training. He was traveling a dead-end road and the end was in sight even before he was thirty years old!

"What are your plans for the future, Bud?" I asked him. "Wouldn't you like to get out of this spot and go on up the ladder?"

"Sure I would," he said. "But I don't know how to go about it."

"Build yourself a blueprint for the future," I told him. "Technically, you're well qualified—*but only about your own operation!* You've got to expand your knowledge, not only about the entire plant, but about outside interests, too. And truthfully, Bud," I said, "you ought to go to night school and take some courses in public speaking, English, and correspondence. You and I both know that your grammar and your spelling are atrocious.

"I'll tell you what, Bud. Let me give you five points for progress and you see if you can't work up your own blueprint for action from them."

Here's what those five points are, just as I gave them to Bud.

Five Pointers for Progress.

1. *Take the initiative.* Don't wait for your company or your boss to tell you what to do to get ahead. You are responsible for development of yourself and your own individual talents.

2. *Seek responsibility.* Actively seek all the responsibility you can possibly handle. Accept it eagerly. Look for it. You'll never get anywhere by avoiding the tough assignments. Adopt the attitude of *the difficult we do at once; the impossible takes a little time.*

3. *Be decisive in your actions.* Develop your ability to make quick decisions. It's easy to say, "Facts first-decisions second," but it doesn't always work out that way. Sometimes an immediate decision is more valuable than one reached after weeks of debating. Learn to develop your intuitive instincts here. Of course, experience helps. As the old army saying goes, "An experienced officer commands by instinct; the inexperienced one has to work at it!"

4. *Take a few chances.* There's another old army saying that only a small thin line exists between a general court martial and the Congressional Medal of Honor. Remember that men who never stick their necks out never become leaders, either.

5. *Broaden your interests.* Although specialization is important, especially in the beginning for you've got to start from somewhere, it's also a proven fact that the higher you go, the more you must know about everybody's business.

Bud's no longer in his twenties, nor is he still in that dead-end job of his. He decided what he wanted, he made up a definite plan to get it, and he's working on it. Now let me tell you about a second case—my own. You see—

I practice what I preach.

When I decided that I wanted to become a professional writer, I sat down and made up a detailed plan of action. I knew that it meant days and weeks, even months and years, of slow grinding preparation. It meant a rigorous program of bringing myself back up to date on grammar, sentence structure, and word usage. And those were only the tools. Of the techniques of writing, I knew absolutely nothing. Here, my gratitude goes to my understanding editors at Parker Publishing Company. Without their help and their patience, I'd never have made it.

But I did study and I worked hard to learn. I knew what I wanted and I knew where I wanted to go. Was I successful in my efforts? The fact that this book exists is evidence in itself. However, you are the final judge of how successfully I've learned my lessons. My point is this: *I had a blueprint for action.* I had a definite timetable to follow and I followed it.

Try Mr. Meyer's five step program for success.

Paul J. Meyer, President of Success Motivation Institute, Incorporated, whom I mentioned in the first few pages of this book, has this to say about blueprint planning and goal achievement.

"1. *Crystallize your thinking*. Determine what specific goal you want to achieve. Then dedicate yourself to its attainment with unswerving singleness of purpose.

"2. *Develop a plan for achieving your goal, and a deadline for its attainment*. Plan your progress carefully—hour-by-hour, day-by-day, month-by-month. Organized activity and maintained enthusiasm are the wellsprings of your power.

"3. *Develop a sincere desire for the things you want*. A burning desire is the greatest motivator of every human action. The desire for success implants *success consciousness* which, in turn, creates a vigorous and ever-increasing *habit of success*.

"4. *Develop supreme confidence in yourself and your own abilities*. Enter every activity without giving mental recognition to the possibility of defeat. Concentrate on your strengths instead of your weaknesses . . . on your powers instead of your problems.

"5. *Develop a dogged determination to follow through on your plan regardless of obstacles, criticism, or circumstances*. Construct your determination with sustained effort, controlled attention, and concentrated energy."

4. Make a man's goal exciting and worth while.

If you want to get a man out of the rut of boredom, make his goal exciting and worthwhile. Although it's true enough that a man will have to figure out what he himself actually wants out of life, you can help him identify that goal. Many times he may see a goal of some sort, but he lacks the imagination to see that goal in relation to himself and his own endeavors to reach it. So it remains elusive, vague, and nebulous to him.

"OK, so I go to night school and study English and grammar and business correspondence," Bud might have said to himself when I suggested it. "So what? What happens then?"

To spell it out to him, had he asked that question, I'd have listed certain tangible benefits that would result from his extra efforts. I'd have said,

"Bud, your efforts will give you at least four benefits that I can think of, and maybe even more. But at any rate, your blueprint for action can give you—

"1. More money—and lots of it.

"2. And with that money—you can get a better home—more material things for yourself, for your wife and your children.

"3. That'll bring you prestige, recognition, and advancement for yourself in your own community.

"4. You'll gain a certain amount of psychic reward, for to learn, to know more than you knew the day before, is worthwhile in itself. To have people come to you for advice, for help, because you know more than they do about something, is definite gratification."

5. Cheer him on from the sidelines.

Ever seen it before? If not, you're not a member of the set who watches it happen every crisp autumn weekend and on into the cold crackle of winter, either as a spectator in the stadium or at home on TV. Of course, it's football; from Mighty-Mites to the mighty pros.

But it's the show on the sidelines I'm talking about now—the cheerleaders. What's the purpose of all their gyrations, their leaps and their bounds, their chanting? It's a special kind of incitement. Their goal is to keep the team's enthusiasm at a fever-pitch! "We want a touchdown!" they scream, and the home team comes through.

"There's all the difference in the world between playing to empty stands and to a packed cheering and yelling stadium," says Bill Bayless, coach at Glendale High. "Take a homecoming game, for example. There's an electric thrill that crackles in the air when the crowd's behind you and cheering you on. The team loves it, and so do the coaches," he laughingly concludes.

Victory without a cheering crowd becomes empty and hollow. So remember this: You can keep your men's enthusiasm at the boiling point, you can get them to give it their all, but only if you continually cheer them on.

Little else need be said here, for this is your job to do—not his, and it's all so simple. *Just cheer for him!*

6. Give them a cause to fight for.

The 442nd became one of the most heroic and most decorated units of World War II. President Roosevelt was laudatory in his praise of these loyal Nisei; these courageous American citizens born of Japanese parents.

These men not only had an emotional rallying point, but they also had a cause to fight for. And they had a tremendous number of cheering spectators through the newspapers, radio, and honest sincere reporters with a heart like Ernie Pyle cheering them on. They truly earned their name—*Go for Broke*, for they did!

It's not easy to do.

"Oh yes," you may say. "It's easy to do in wartime. It's a lot harder to do in peacetime." Sorry, I can't agree with you. What about Joseph Pirone and Thomas Edison? Or a hundred others I might name? *It's not easy to do at any time!* But that's what makes the game worthwhile. If it were easy to get your men to go for broke—everybody could do it! That's where your initiative, your ingenuity, and your executive skill come into play. You can do it, too, if you use these—

Memory joggers.

1. *Appeal to a man's emotions; establish an emotional rallying point,* and you'll win the victory in spite of the odds against you.

2. *Give them a goal to shoot for.* They'll push you and your company to the top while they're reaching it.

3. *Give them a blueprint for action,* and you'll get every man to be his own self-starter.

4. *Make his goal exciting and worthwhile,* and you'll get him out of his rut of apathy and boredom.

5. *Cheer him on from the sidelines,* and you'll keep his enthusiasm at a fever-pitch.

6. *Give your men a cause to fight for, and they'll GO FOR BROKE for you!*

THE 7TH SECRET

Emphasize Skill — Not Rules

Once upon a time there was a very obedient soldier named Smith. One day when Smith's World War II division was in Louisiana on maneuvers, his sergeant stationed him at a lonely road intersection and told him to direct traffic. Smith was instructed not to leave his post until he was properly relieved.

Three days later, when a temporary cessation of the mock hostilities had been declared, Smith's sergeant realized he was missing one man in his squad—namely, Smith.

Jumping into a jeep, he hurried to the road intersection where he'd left Smith. Sure enough, Smith was still there, but he was directing *civilian* traffic—not military. Hungry? Famished. Thirsty? Of course. But he'd remained faithfully at his post, never questioning his orders.

Division officers asked Smith if he hadn't felt something could be wrong, especially when the military traffic he'd been told to direct abruptly stopped and was replaced by civilian cars.

"Yes sir," he said. "I thought something might be wrong, but I figured it was none of my business. My sergeant told me not to leave my post until I was properly relieved. And sir—I just hadn't been properly relieved!"

Smith's officers gave up questioning him when they heard that. It was no further use. *Smith believed he was right just as long as he followed the rules.*

Diligence is not always a virtue.

Were his actions commendable? Yes, in a sense, if a man is to be praised for *blindly following the rules without question.* But diligence and dullness don't go together. After missing two meals in a row, I would have been finding out exactly where my relief was and why he hadn't shown up to replace me!

But I was never one to go too much by the rules just for the sake of following the rules when I was in the army, especially if they didn't make any sense.

Rules for the sake of rules isn't confined to the military.

One morning I stood with a young foreman watching the change of shifts in his department. It was a few minutes before seven—the plant time for punching out on the time clock. The day shift had already reported; they'd been briefed about their current production by the outgoing crew. Ready and waiting at their machines, they needed only their supervisor's nod to start up.

The outgoing shift was tired. They'd been on duty since eleven the night before. Now that they were through, they were squatting on their haunches, or sitting on stacks of rubber skids waiting for the seven o'clock whistle to blow.

The young foreman called his shift supervisor over. "Get those men on their feet," he said. "You know I don't allow anyone to sit down while he's working in my department!"

"But sir," the supervisor protested. "These men are all through work. They're just waiting to go home."

"Don't talk back to me! That's an order!" the foreman snapped. "They're still on the clock so get 'em on their feet! *Those are my rules!*"

Rule by work — not by rules.

If you've ever been guilty of such conduct, remember that you should *rule by work; don't work by rules.* Later on, I'll give you eight principles to follow when you make up your own rules. The purpose of these principles is to guide you toward your goal—the accomplishment of your primary mission—*to make a profit.* That's the purpose of rules, too.

If the rules you make in your company or your department aren't directing your efforts toward that ultimate goal—*making a profit*—you'd better take another look at them, or your company might not be there the next time you do.

Not everybody in the military is rule-happy.

This foreman is much like the battalion commander who insisted on keeping his men out in a blizzard just because the Army Training Program called for a week's bivouac in the seventh week of basic training.

He had the authority to cancel the bivouac, but he wouldn't. He was a stickler for *following the rules.* If the ATP called for a one week bivouac, then, by golly, they'd have a one week bivouac—blizzard or no blizzard!

But his regimental commander took a much different viewpoint toward rules and regulations. Most army officers read regulations with the approach of—*if it doesn't say I can—then I can't!*

Not Colonel Richmond. *"If it doesn't say I can't—then I can!"* he said. "So bring your battalion in, Major. There's no sense in bivouacking in the middle of a snowstorm. It only takes 24 hours to learn how to be miserable!"

What benefits will be yours by not following the rules?

When you emphasize skill—not rules—you'll harvest a crop of P's—the *Four P's of Production*—

PEAK PERFORMANCE for PEAK PROFITS.

You'll receive these specific benefits. Well worth throwing away the rulebook for, aren't they? Now don't worry; I know I told you a few moments ago I'd give you some principles to follow in making up your rules, so we're not going to give up all rules completely. I know there must be some, too! And if you do insist on keeping them right now, here are eight you can follow to get those Four P's of Production by emphasizing skill!

1. *Give him a job to do and let him do it.*
2. *Urge your employee to use his skill, his initiative, and his ingenuity to beat your established standards.*
3. *Offer him security in return for his knowledge when he translates his know-how into skills on the job for you.*
4. *Urge him to set up his own goals and establish his own standards of performance.*
5. *Let him work in his own style.*
6. *Set up a system to test an employee for his maximum potential.*
7. *Let him tell you how and where he needs to improve.*
8. *Let him recommend ways of improving work methods on his job.*

Now let's see how others have harvested the Four P's of Production—Peak Performance for Peak Profits—by using these methods, and how you can do it, too.

1. Give him a job to do and let him do it.

You should be interested in results—not methods. As long as the accomplishment of the mission doesn't infringe upon the welfare of your employees, you should not care how the job is done—just as long as it's done! I've never found a better example of this principle than in this true story I want to tell you now.

No accidents — no lectures!

The commander of Kadena Air Force Base in Okinawa, a full bird colonel, was in hot water with his superiors because of the high accident rate on his base. In the daily chewing-out session of his base safety officer, the colonel made it clear that unless this situation improved rapidly, the base safety officer was going to be out of a job—not only as safety officer, but in the entire air force!

In a frenzy of activity, the safety officer scheduled safety lectures almost every hour. Safety films were shown in the theaters instead of the latest movies fresh from stateside. These were shown during the most accident-prone part of the week—Saturday and Sunday afternoons and evenings. Compulsory attendance? Naturally!

Passes and leaves were cancelled. Airmen were restricted to the base; drivers' licenses were revoked and suspended. Every precaution was taken to prevent an accident. The base was living in a sea of safety slogans; they were plastered on every wall. The command was knee-deep in a veritable flood of lectures; millions of words on safety had been spoken. The safety officer had followed every possible rule in the book; but the accidents kept right on happening!

Then, close to a state of panic himself, the colonel relieved the safety officer and appointed the newest second lieutenant from the states to the job. That young officer, a fighter pilot anxious to be in the air over the East China Sea on patrol duty, was disgusted with this ground assignment. The commander assured him that as soon as the crisis was over—he would be immediately restored to flying duty.

In less than two weeks—the lieutenant was back in the colonel's office; twenty-four hours after he'd taken over, the accidents had stopped. The rate was down to zero.

"How did you do it?" the colonel asked, astounded at the lieutenant's performance.

"Simple, sir," the lieutenant said. "I figured if the safety officer had been going by the rules—the rules must be wrong. So I stopped everything he'd been doing. I assembled all the men and held one meeting with them. It lasted less than thirty seconds; I spoke only five words. I said, 'Gentlemen, *no accidents—no lectures!*' "

2. Urge your employee to use his skill, his initiative, and his ingenuity to beat your established standards.

Wage incentive plans on a production line work for the employee just like a salary plus commission for a salesman. The wage incentive system stimulates a man's thinking. Once a quota is set and a standard of performance is fixed, then your employees will use their ingenuity and their skills to beat your system. They'll produce more so they can earn more incentive pay.

You can motivate a man if you'll challenge him to beat your system. Tax his initiative. When he succeeds, reward him generously with money and praise. The principle is excellent and practical, says Barney Clayton, the controller with Dayco's plant in Springfield, Missouri.

"Here at Springday we've learned that the only worthwhile system for us is the incentive plan," says Barney. "Our industrial engineering department sets realistic production figures for every job in the plant with time and motion studies. Our accounting department breaks it down into dollars and cents so it represents a good day's pay for the man. *That's his salary*. He gets that for each day's work even if the machinery's broken down and he produces nothing. What he produces above that base figure is *his commission*. We've seen our plant production figures nearly double since we've used this system.

"Oh, we have a few who want to coast along on the *salary figure*. They don't last. Most of our operations are on a team basis; if a man keeps his teammate from earning more money, they get rid of him themselves."

I've seen the operation at Springday (Dayco's subsidiary in Springfield) and it works. It must be good; Springday is the world's largest producer of V-belts. And production is increasing every year; they've added a new research and development building, and they're expanding their industrial belt division, too.

3. Offer a man security in return for his knowledge when he translates his know-how into skills on the job for you.

The average man spends his money—after he's taken care of his basic necessities such as food, clothing, and shelter—to buy security and independence, approval and recognition, recreation and self-satisfaction.

"Offer a man these things as well as money; he'll work just that much harder for you," says Dr. Elbert Johnson, economics professor at Drury College. "If a man will spend money to gain self-satisfaction and to feed his ego off the job—think how much more effective he'll be for you if you give him those things on the job!"

Of course, the real feeling of security in a man's work comes when he knows that he's respected by you; and that he's both liked and wanted; that you think highly of his efforts for you. To get him to feel that way, emphasize skill—not rules.

4. Get him to set up his own goals and establish his own standards.

It takes initiative to set your own goals; it requires skill and ingenuity to reach them. Selling is a lot like picking apples. It's easy to stand on the ground and strip the low branches. Anyone can do that. It takes some effort to get the apples at the top of the tree.

Real goals are set by the salesman.

"It isn't enough for a company to set its own sales goals," says Sam Hayward, a Division Manager for Sears. "The average good salesman will meet those minimum goals. He has to if he wants to keep his job.

"The real goals are set only when he sets his own. Sure they should be realistic. If he sets his target too high and misses his mark too far, he'll get discouraged and quit. He should fix a sensible goal he can reach in a reasonable time. Naturally, that goal would have to be higher than the one Sears has already set."

5. Let a man work in his own style.

"I doubt if there's a job in all the world where a man will not be able to express his own personality in some way," says Dr. William Schneider, psychology professor at Logan College. Dr. Schneider felt strongly about this. I've seen him peel down to his T-shirt in the classroom to illustrate his point. Of course, St. Louis can be cruelly hot and humid in the late spring and early summer months!

Certain jobs lend themselves more to personal expression than do others. Teaching, selling, painting, writing, any profession or occupation that is creative in nature, allows a style of individual expression often denied to the man on the production line or at the work bench. It's the responsibility of management to help that man express his own individuality.

If you can, give that man the right to do his own job in his own way as long as the end results meet your requirements. It might be such a simple thing as letting a man use a stool rather than stand or letting the janitor make the decision about which end of the building to sweep first. Help each man find ways of pouring his own personality into his job; you'll motivate him to be a far better employee when you do.

6. Set up a system to test an employee for his maximum potential.

Take civil service employment, for instance. It isn't enough that a man barely pass a civil service exam for federal employment. The U.S. government is interested in finding out *which man is best qualified for the job.*

When a new position is created or a vacancy occurs because of promotion or retirement, the federal register is checked for the top three names on that list based on the examination results. These three people are interviewed; the best one is selected. The other two names go back on the top of the register again. This insures our government of getting people who have demonstrated their maximum potential. It helps get rid of political pork barrel worthless employees.

Try this method of promotion.

Daniel North, executive vice-president of General Development, was retiring. The question: who should take his place? He was concerned about this problem, so about a month or so before he retired, he wrote to the president of the corporation to make this suggestion.

"I know two good men who are capable of filling my position. I don't know which is better. I suggest you promote both of them to positions of divisional vice-presidents. Put one in charge of sales; the other in charge of development.

"Leave my position vacant. These men are good friends. They'll be in competition for my position and they'll both know it. But because of their deep friendship, they'll compete honestly and competently. Their competition will help the company. After a period of close observation, promote the one you think is better qualified for my job. In the end, all will gain."

7. Let a man tell you how and where he needs to improve.

"Criticizing a man will destroy his initiative, his ingenuity, and his will to work," says David Spencer, one of the more than 300 branch office managers with Snelling and Snelling, Inc., a world-wide employment counseling service. "We see case after case where employees—including a lot of top-level management people—have quit their jobs because of excessive and unwarranted criticism."

I'm not saying that criticism isn't worthwhile and that it doesn't have its place. I do feel that criticism accomplishes its purpose only if a person is allowed to criticize himself. Then it can be used as a true motivator for self-improvement.

Here's a system you can use . . .

Every three months, more often if necessary, have your supervisors hold a counseling session with each subordinate. Let him tell the employees about their *good points*. Then let each employee enumerate his own *weak points*. The session usually ends with a commitment from the employee to improve. He's sincere about it, too.

You'll find he will usually improve. A person hates to come back into the boss's office three months later and recite off those same bad points all over again.

8. Let him recommend ways of improving the methods on his own job.

"I found out a long time ago that to ask a man for generalized suggestions for improvement was a complete waste of time," says Jack Hurley, head of the industrial belt division with Gates Rubber. "But I didn't know how to get the specifics out of him until I started using the checklist you gave me, Jim.

"Now I have my supervisors go over this checklist with the employee any time one of them has an idea about how to improve his work methods. It works real well for us; we've gotten good results from it."

This checklist I gave to Jack is a six step process you can use to get your employee's job improvement suggestions down in writing.

JOB IMPROVEMENT CHECKLIST

1. Have your employee prepare in writing a detailed, step-by-step description of exactly how the job is being done now. This will force him to think—to be sure of what

he's saying. Talking about improvement and getting it down in concrete and specific terms on paper are two different things.

2. Have your employee question every detail of his present operation with the five W's,

Who,
    What,
        When,
            Where,
                Why (How).

3. Next, have him work out his proposed changes in writing showing in detail *how* it's going to work, *where* it differs from the old system, and *why* it's important to make this change.

Follow the basic premise that any change in present operation must result in a saving of time, manpower, or material. There must be an increase in either quantity or quality and an increased profit for the company. *This should also mean an increase in base salary for the employee.* Lacking that incentive—the system won't work!

4. If there's the slightest indication these proposed changes will bring about an improvement, the fourth step is your responsibility. After the details have been worked out, go to your superior and get permission to put the plan into operation—usually on a 30 to 90 day trial basis.

5. If you get the OK from your boss (or if you're the boss) then explain the improved method to everyone affected by it. Get everybody into the act so they'll know what's going on. Sometimes you'll get a plan this far only to have it shot down in flames by an employee who catches something everyone else has missed.

6. Put the improved plan into operation. Watch it carefully to make sure everything is working properly. You'll always find some bugs to get rid of. And you can bet your plant manager, the controller, and your production superintendent will all be monitoring your new procedure, too.

EIGHT PRINCIPLES FOR RULE-MAKING

1. Every rule should be aimed at accomplishment of your primary mission.

A rule that doesn't help you do your main job—*earn a profit* for your company—is a worthless rule. Whenever you make a new rule, keep the Four P's of Production in mind—Peak Performance for Peak Profits.

2. A good rule should consider the welfare of your employees.

Most rules and regulations about safety come under this principle. If a man should wear safety goggles or heavy gloves or safety shoes because of the hazards of his job—then that's a good rule to make and enforce. You'll find your people are interested in their own welfare; no man wants to lose a hand or an eye or a foot. Once the employees of a department know what rules of safety are best for them, they'll enforce those rules even more effectively than will their own supervisor.

3. A good rule should raise the morale of your employees.

Moderate griping about the situation doesn't always indicate low morale. It's human nature. In small doses, griping can serve as a good safety valve for your employees. Don't let it get out of hand, but remember that without some dissatisfaction, there'd be no incentive to do things in a better way.

4. Esprit is an important indicator of the soundness of your rules.

Any outfit that's overburdened with red tape and useless regulations will have a low esprit. Your rulebook and your administrative procedures should be kept as sparkling, clean, and up to date as your equipment.

5. Good rules make for good discipline.

If your men promptly obey your orders and willingly follow your instructions, you're in fine shape. If they take the proper action in the absence of orders—don't touch a thing! It's almost too good to be true.

6. Rules should help improve a man's individual job proficiency.

Safety is your guiding factor, but don't go overboard to the point a man can't produce until he's triple-checked every nut and bolt and filled out seventeen safety forms in quintuplicate before he dares turn on the motor. Rules should help a man do his job—not hinder him.

7. Every rule should be aimed at improving your organizational efficiency.

Men are proficient—organizations are efficient, just as morale is singular and esprit is plural. A regulation that's good for the production line, but poor for the shipping department shouldn't be enforced for the whole plant. Use the seventh principle to establish broad organizational policy rather than writing individual rules and regulations for departments.

8. The most effective rules are those your employees make to discipline their own conduct.

Not every barracks thief in the army gets a court-martial. Some aren't physically capable of walking to the trial after the kangaroo court held in the company. When you want to enforce a rule that punishes the entire group for the mistakes of one individual—remember this eighth principle. Without a doubt, your employees have already taken corrective action of their own!

Whenever you make a rule—check it out against these eight principles of rule-making. Even if it passes all eight tests with flying colors, remember that—

Rules are made to be broken.

"Rules are made to be broken," says E. Richard Johns, business consultant for Zenith, Sears, and a host of other industrial and commercial giants. "Ask any teen-ager. Or what about you? Do you always drive within the speed limit when the road's straight and clear, the air's crisp, the sky's blue, and there's not a cop in sight anywhere?

"Well, your employees are no different than you are. If you emphasize rules just for the sake of rules, or if you insist on doing it by the book that's completely outdated and been gathering dust on the shelf for 20 years—stand back and watch the circus! That's all you'll have; you'll not have a business."

Dick is right. When you emphasize rules—and not skill—you fall into the bad habit of passing the buck. You find yourself answering an employee's question of "Why?" with "Because *they* said so!" What kind of an answer is that? Who are *they*?

Or is your answer "It's always been done this way before!" Why has it always been done this way? Is it the best way? Is it perfect? Couldn't it be improved on just a bit? Or is it just another of those musty ironclad rules you drag up when you want to slap a man down or evade the real issue?

Those answers make about as much sense as the women's group in a church that meets in order to raise money to meet the budget so they can have a place to meet to raise money to meet the budget!

In the final analysis.

1. Always judge your employee's actions and his procedures by the end results—both in terms of increasing the competitive position of your company and the self-satisfaction of the man.

2. Go easy on the pat rules unless it has to do with safety. Doing it by the book isn't always the best way. If an off-the-wall solution works and makes those who use it more satisfied with their work, use it! Don't throw it out because it's never been done or because you didn't think of it first.

3. Don't answer an employee's suggestion with "*They* said it has to be done *this way*!" You're only passing the buck!

If you do want peak performance for peak profits, follow these eight guidelines—

1. *Give a man a job to do and let him do it.*

2. *Urge your employee to use his skill, his initiative, and his ingenuity to beat your established standards.*

3. *Offer him security in return for his knowledge when he translates his know-how into skills on the job for you.*

4. *Get him to set up his own goals and establish his own standards of performance.*

5. *Let him work in his own style.*

6. *Set up a system to test an employee for his maximum potential.*

7. *Let him tell you how and where he needs to improve.*

8. *Let him recommend ways of improving work methods on his job.*

"I'm not interested in methods—I'm interested in results!" said General George S. Patton, famed commander of World War II. "If you want to win—you've got to use skill, guts, determination, perseverance, initiative, ingenuity, and a dozen other fine qualities of leadership. But above all—you've got to throw away the rulebook!"

And General Patton's results speak for themselves. While other generals (on both sides) were fighting by the rulebook of World War I, *General Patton was writing a new one!* When he fought, the so-called rules of conventional warfare went flying out the window.

He wrote his own rules and he won; so can you!

How to Say It with Flowers!

"To be a good critic demands more brains and judgment than most men possess," said Josh Billings. Criticism is what we say about other people who don't have the same faults that we have. Or as the Chinese would put it: Those who have free seats always hiss first.

What is a critic, really? The dictionary says a critic is a person who makes judgments of the merits and faults (mainly the faults, I'm sure) of books, music, pictures, plays, acting. You might think of a critic as a person who gets paid for finding fault with something someone else has said or done. I have yet to meet the writer who honestly likes a literary critic. I personally have my own opinion. I put a critic in the same class as a legless man who teaches running.

No one likes to be criticized. No one wants to be told that he is wrong, that he's made a mistake. Criticism has the potential power to destroy a good employee and make him worthless to you. It is one of man's deadliest weapons. Unless a person has a completely sadistic outlook on life, he does not enjoy criticizing another individual.

But there will be times when you have no other choice; there's no other way out. Sometimes not to criticize, to overlook an error, is far worse than to discipline and to punish the man. And criticism is a form of punishment; no doubt about it. So you might as well accept the fact that at times you must reprimand, you must criticize, you must punish.

That's one of the penalties you pay for being a supervisor—an executive—a manager. But you ought to be able to handle the situation gracefully. You ought to know how to say it with flowers. That's why this chapter is in this book—to show you how.

Most people feel that a person isn't going to improve unless he's criticized and shown where he's making his mistake. This could be true—but only if you substitute the word *guide* for criticism.

Before you criticize or find fault with any employee, always ask yourself these three important questions:

    1. *Am I just criticizing or am I actually guiding and counseling this man?*

      2. *What advantages will become mine when I criticize him?*

        3. *What benefits will I gain by criticizing him?*

You must gain the benefits.

Follow the principle that *you must obtain the end benefits* that come out of any counseling session. If you're not getting the end advantage, you might as well forget about it. Your criticism isn't worthwhile. In fact, it'll probably do you more harm than good.

If you can honestly see where a guidance session with one of your employees will improve his production performance—that's to your advantage. Do it. If you can see increased profits (or savings—remember the principles of good salesmanship) coming from your criticism, do so; that's to your benefit, too, and well worth it.

And speaking of profit, I've often heard it said that most of the money a businessman calls profit is money that hasn't been foolishly spent. So keep your eye on the back door, too. You might plug some profit leaks with counseling sessions about excessive waste.

If you're looking for benefits from criticism of your employees, remember *the Four P's of Production* that I told you about in the last chapter—*Peak Performance for Peak Profits.* When criticizing your men, keep these Four P's of Production in mind.

Production should be your primary interest, no matter whether it's sales production or factory production. Even a farmer is interested in production. If your criticism helps your *productions, performance, and profits,* you're on the right track. Go ahead and criticize!

Getting angry with an employee hurts you — not him; and it isn't criticism!

"I used to run my department like a cop handing out traffic tickets," says Arnold Willis of Reynolds Aluminum. "I'd been given the idea by a tough old supervisor that I had to keep on a man's tail every minute to keep him working. If I gave a guy a break, I thought I was being a pansy.

"Well, I ended up in the hospital for three weeks on a Sippy diet—a glass of half and half every hour on the hour and nothing but amphojel in between. It didn't take my doctor long to diagnose my problem either. In less than a week I was trying to run that hospital like my department. I was chewing out everyone in sight. When they didn't listen, I got all the madder at them.

"At my last consultation before I was discharged, my doctor said, 'You're giving yourself your own ulcers; your employees didn't give them to you at all. Neither did your boss or the business. Let me give you a little tip. It doesn't matter to the other fellow how much you hate him. It doesn't hurt him one bit. It only hurts you. So ease off, my friend, ease off. Live and let live.'

"I tried it; I had to. That was over four years ago. I haven't had an ulcer attack since. And incidentally, I'm no longer a department foreman," he grinned. "I've been promoted!"

Let's get right down to specifics. I'm going to give you sixteen steps you can follow to correct your employee's mistakes without offending him; sixteen steps to criticize him constructively and not be hated for it.

1. *Call attention to a person's mistakes indirectly.* (Do this, and you'll do away with the requirement for a formal counseling session in 95 percent of your problem cases.)

2. Find out all the pertinent facts.
3. Decide whether formal criticism is needed or not.
4. If it is—you pick the time and place.
5. Never lose your temper with an employee.
6. Always begin with sincere praise and honest appreciation.
7. Take your own inventory as well as his.
8. Give your employee plenty of chance to talk.
9. Weigh all the evidence and the facts carefully.
10. If punishment is a must, fit it to both the crime and the individual.
11. Let a man select his own punishment.
12. Close your interview with sincere praise and honest appreciation.
13. Praise the slightest improvement and praise every improvement.
14. Give your employee a high reputation to live up to.
15. Follow up with a second interview—if necessary.
16. Don't criticize too often.

From the beginning . . . .

1. Call attention to a person's mistakes indirectly.

One of the goals of criticism should be to prevent a recurrence of the same mistake. If you can do that by the use of this step alone—you'll not have to go on into the formal steps of criticism.

When you see that something's wrong, when you see a mistake being made, simply walk over to the group and ask, *"What happened?"* That's all! The cardinal rule to remember here is to *leave out all personal remarks.* Don't pinpoint anyone by name. When you ask, "What happened?", you get rid of personalities completely. *You bore down on the mistake itself, and only on the mistake.*

How it works.

"Here's how I use this method," says Ralph Snow, safety inspector for Pan American World Airways. "I might say, 'Funny—we've never had any trouble with this machine before—*what happened?*' 'This is the first accident like this—*what happened?*' 'I've never seen plastic do that before—*what happened?*'

"By asking what happened—I'm not blaming anyone. I'm not hunting a culprit. I'm simply looking for facts. And it works. Even when the person who's at fault is found, it takes off the sharp edge; it gets rid of the bite. Just compare these two statements: *What happened? Who did it?* You can even feel the difference!"

You can figure out how to use this step in your own operation. The two important words to remember are: *What happened?* Get your men to open up and talk. Get them to tell you what went wrong. All you need do is listen.

2. Get all the pertinent facts.

If you can get all the facts together by asking what happened—fine. You might be able to solve your problem right there. Sometimes, however, your men won't come right out and give you all the straight answers, *especially when you're at fault*.

Sometimes the mistake comes from poor instructions, improper orders, bad rules, misassignments. Management pulls some boners, too, but few employees want to tell the boss when he's wrong. To do so can invite devastating retaliation in some cases.

Tell your boss what he has to hear.

"Whenever one of my subordinates has the courage to tell me I'm wrong, I know I've found a man who's capable of accepting greater responsibility," says Joe Maxon of Republic Steel. "So many of our young management people are afraid to do that. Of course, it depends on their boss's attitude; I know that, too.

"That's why I've always tried to maintain the policy with my staff of 'Don't tell me what I'd like to hear; *tell me what I have to hear!*' "

3. Decide whether formal criticism is needed or not.

"I doubt if there's a foreman in all the world who honestly likes to dish out criticism," says Paul Holland, a shop foreman with Borg-Warner. "But it's part of your supervisory responsibility.

"You may think you're getting along in good shape in your department. Men doing their jobs and doing them well. Then something goes wrong. Someone may break a rule—maybe cause an accident—become careless in his work. Then the honeymoon's over. Disciplinary action is called for in a hurry—*from you*—whether you like it or not.

"Since there's so much machinery and so many electrical shop fixtures in my department, I always try to push the safety angle when I find one of my men doing something wrong. I try to figure out an approach that'll stress safety and still get the job done. But if that doesn't do the trick, we head for my office where we can deal out the real cards on the table."

Discipline can mean criticism and vice-versa, but seldom does discipline alone teach a man. True discipline must not only punish, *it must also correct*. And your criticism must be constructive, or it's not needed.

If it's constructive—no doubt it's necessary. If you're interested only in *revenge*, if you want to *get even*, or perhaps, *save your own face*, it's not. Constructive criticism should teach an employee to discipline himself; his self-discipline should be your ultimate goal.

4. If formal criticism is necessary — you pick the time and the place.

The biggest advantage of being the attacker in war is that you choose your own time and place of battle. And so it is here. Barring an emergency, your criticism must be done in private. Sometimes you'll not have that chance. You'll have to take immediate action to save a life, prevent serious injury, or save valuable equipment. Other than that, complete privacy is a must.

Reprimands in the presence of other employees cause humiliation and deep resentment instead of creating a desire in the man to do better in the future. So keep it on a man-to-man basis away from prying eyes and overeager ears. Give the man a chance to save face, too. It's important to Caucasians as well as Orientals; employees as well as employers.

If possible, hold your interview in a quiet place. If you and your employee have to shout at each other, there's always a further chance for more misunderstanding. People become excited in noise and confusion. Yell at a man and he'll misinterpret noise for anger.

5. Never lose your temper with an employee.

It's best never to lose your temper with an employee. Above all, never do so in a counseling session. If you do, you'll end up with nothing but a hot-tempered argument between two angry people. You won't even be able to remember the point of the interview.

If you can't see any other good results except for your temporarily feeling better for having blown off steam, don't do it. You're a human being, not a radiator. Don't let personal feelings and personal opinion creep into your daily work. That's the "Smith, you ought to part your hair on the other side" kind of criticism. It's useless.

That kind of criticism will go in one ear and out the other—if you're lucky. If your employee remembers any of it, he'll only recall that you lost your temper, that you were sarcastic, or that you criticized him unjustly when he didn't really have it coming.

A baseball manager or a baseball coach has to turn a deaf ear to criticism most of the time. As Casey Stengel once put it, "I sure could use a guy who could play every position perfectly, never strike out, or never make an error. Trouble is—I can't get him to put down his hot dog and come out of the stands!"

6. Always begin with sincere praise and honest admiration.

Never blast a man off his feet the moment he comes into your office. Don't list all his defects of character one after another. Few of us live who can take that kind of punishment for long. Tell him how good he is, how much you think of him, what a good job he's been doing, *all except for this one small point* you want to talk over with him . . . .

All of us hunger for a word of praise. Everyone likes a compliment. As Mark Twain once said, "I can live for two months on one good compliment." *So praise first; criticize second; praise in the end again.* Sprinkle your criticism with a lot of *TLC—tender loving care.*

7. Take your own inventory, too.

You don't have to list all your mistakes for the past ten years to follow this rule. George Ralston with the 3M Corporation does this. "Here's the way I handle it," he says. "I start out by saying, 'John, I've done the same thing myself before, and a lot more times than you have, too! Here's what I did to correct my mistake.' Then I tell him how I managed to do it—which really is an easy way of letting him know what I want him to do—and then I ask him if he'll give it a whirl my way. What else can he say except that he'll give it a try—and he does, too."

8. Give the man plenty of chance to talk.

If you'll ask a few leading questions, you can usually get a man to open up and talk. He's always anxious to give you the low-down if you'll just ask him for it. Give him a chance to unload all his problems and you should be able to uncover the real reason for his mistake. Do that, and you'll be in a much better position to help him—and yourself, too—by taking action to prevent this mistake from happening again.

9. Weigh all the evidence and the facts carefully.

Before you ever enter into a formal counseling period, you should have gathered enough information to warrant it. However, more information may come to light now that wasn't available before. It might be that since you've seen your employee's side of the picture, you find that no corrective action is needed. If so, *close your interview* promptly and pleasantly.

Handle this properly and your employee need never know that he was suspect for some specific mistake. "Whenever I'm in doubt and I have to call a fellow in, I start out this way," says John McCall of Oxford Industries, Inc. "I tell him of a problem that's on my mind; then I ask him for his advice or for his opinion.

"For example, one time we were having a tremendously high rate of small tool pilferage. We narrowed it down to three or four suspects. I called them in one at a time and talked to them about *my* problem. As an excuse for having the man in my office, I told him I needed his help—I wanted his expert advice on the punishment to be given. I implied throughout we knew who the thief was. I only wanted his valuable opinion.

"I talked to each man the same way. The pilferage stopped. I don't know to this day who was guilty. I don't care. It might have been one of the men I interviewed—maybe not. If not, the factory grapevine carried my message to the guilty party. The point is, not only was my problem solved, but some man's job and reputation were saved, too."

10. Fit the punishment both to the crime and the individual.

The purpose of punishment should be to correct—nothing more. Take our penitentiaries for example. *They are supposed to be corrective institutions.* The most progressive ones are. When a prisoner of theirs is freed, he's usually ready to become a useful member of society.

If the penitentiary (guided by state policy) has only punishment in mind, a released man is usually interested only in *revenge* and in *getting even* with society for putting him there.

These same two methods are found in industry; there seems to be no middle road. When the wrong disciplinary methods are used—when the man feels that he's been treated unfairly—you have a petty criminal on your hands.

I know a certain factory (the name, I'll not mention) that uses *punishment for the sake of punishment.* They go far beyond the practice of rules for the sake of rules. And their employees hate management. Willful destruction of company property is common; theft is a major problem. So is employee turnover. There is no loyalty whatever. The company could easily double their profits—perhaps even more—if they'd only treat their production employees like human beings.

11. Let a man choose his own punishment.

Ask a man what he thinks you ought to do in his case. You'd be surprised how many will face the situation realistically and honestly. Nine times out of ten they'll give themselves the maximum punishment! *Then you can become their benefactor by reducing the punishment you didn't give them!*

If he goes too easy on himself, tell him you're sorry, but that's not quite what you had in mind. Then tell him what his punishment *has* to be. Even though it's more than he thought he should have, you'll find he'll still accept it with good grace. This happens very rarely, however. Most men will give themselves a more severe sentence than you had in mind.

Put the monkey right on his back.

"I had a basic training company in Fort Riley, Kansas, right after the Korean Conflict ended," says Leo Salter, an executive with Atlas Corporation. "I had a standing rule in the outfit that any man who didn't pass his fifth week proficiency test didn't get a weekend pass. Everyone worked hard to pass it for there were only two weekend passes given during the eight week basic training cycle.

"Around the first part of the fifth week, one of the trainees, who'd gotten married just before his induction, told me his wife was coming down from Wisconsin for his weekend pass.

" 'That's fine,' I said. 'I hope she doesn't make the trip in vain; remember you've got to pass your fifth week test first. If you flunk it, no pass!'

" 'I'll pass it,' he said, but he didn't. He flunked it cold. So there he was on Friday afternoon, a wife who'd come all the way down from Wisconsin sitting in the company area, and no weekend pass!

"I called him into the orderly room. 'You knew my policy,' I said. 'You knew it long before your wife drove down here. What do you want me to do? If I allow you to leave the post, I'll have to give a pass to every other soldier who failed the test, too.

" 'You get behind my desk and sit in my chair. I'm going to the mess hall and have a cup of coffee. For fifteen minutes you're the captain commanding this company—not me. When I come back, you give me your answer. I'll abide by your decision.'

"I didn't get back to the orderly room. In less than ten minutes he was in the mess hall. 'Captain, you're right,' he said. 'I can't give myself a pass to go into town—wife or no wife!'

"He'd made the right decision. I was proud of him. He didn't go into town, but he and his wife had a ball that weekend anyway. I had them put up in the best guesthouse on the post and they were special guests of mine at the club. I've never forgotten that experience. I still use the principle today.

"I'm not quite sure why it works. I'm no psychologist. I don't know whether the motive that moves a man is pride, a sense of duty, or what, but I know this. It works; I don't care how or why."

12. Close your interview with sincere praise and honest appreciation.

Don't end your counseling session on a sour note. Mix some honey with the vinegar. Criticism should leave a person with the idea that he's been helped—not kicked. When you criticize a man, do it with the thought of being helpful—not with the idea of nagging him. As Bernard Baruch once said, "There are two things that are bad for the heart—running upstairs and running down people."

13. Praise the slightest improvement and praise every improvement.

No man can live on a solid diet of criticism. Have you a son? If you have, and he's still in those tender years of grade school, watch his face the next time he brings his report card to you. Suppose you look at it, and say, "Johnny, you didn't do well in reading, did you? In fact, that's a pretty miserable grade!" Watch his reaction. His face will drop; there'll be tears in his eyes. To bring the sunshine back in his face, just say, "But your grades sure went up in spelling and arithmetic. I'm so proud of you!"

If you want the best from your employees, praise the slightest improvement and praise every improvement. As Charles Schwab said, "There is nothing else that so kills the ambitions of a man as criticism from his superiors. So I am anxious to praise but loath to find fault. If I like anything, I am hearty in my approbation and lavish in my praise."

What about you?

14. Give your employee a high reputation to live up to.

If you practice the preceding step, this one will become automatic. Whenever you praise a man, he'll want more of the same. You'll be giving him a reputation to live up to when you compliment him on his work. Set a high standard for a man; he'll know when he's missed it. You'll not have to tell him. If you set no standard for him—he'll aim at nothing. Jose Iturbi said, "The only time you realize you have a reputation is when you're not living up to it."

15. Follow up with a second interview — if necessary.

If another interview is required, harsher methods will be needed. In the first interview all you should do is *plant the seed.* In the second one, it's time to *plow out some weeds.* And if you need still a third interview, then it's high time to *harvest the crop!* If it takes a fourth one—my friend, you just don't have a green thumb!

Three interviews with an employee remind me of the couple who'd been happily married for fifty years. In fact—it was said they'd never had a quarrel. Not one harsh word had been spoken between them. A reporter was interviewing them on their golden wedding anniversary. He asked them for their secret of happiness.

"Well, we left for our honeymoon driving a horse and buggy," the wife said. "Down the road a ways, the horse stumbled. John stopped and said to the horse, 'That's once.' Later, the horse stumbled again, and John said, more harshly this time, 'That's twice!'

"Then the horse stumbled the third time, and John said, 'That's three times!' And he pulled out his pistol and shot the horse dead!

"Well, I looked at John for a moment, and I said, 'John, you shouldn't have done that!' He looked me straight in the eye, blew the smoke from the pistol barrel, and said, *'That's once!'*

"We've never had an argument since that day."

So should be the sequence of your interviews. I've used that story to good effect with employees many a time—both management and labor. It makes my point crystal clear.

16. Don't criticize too often!

Do this, and you'll leave the high level of constructive and helpful criticism to descend to *nagging.* Be a supervisor—not a fishwife. Be moderate in all things.

Highlights.

I'm not going to list these sixteen steps of constructive criticism for you here again. You can refer to them easily by turning back to page 78. Here, I'd like to mention just a few highlights once more.

Get all the facts, review them with those concerned and reach an agreement on them. Then be ready to suggest a constructive course of action for the future. When you criticize, concentrate on the methods or the results—not on the personalities. If you can preface your criticism with a bit of honest praise, do so. If you can't—*invent some.*

Always find a private place to criticize an employee. Criticizing him in the presence of others undermines his morale, his self-confidence, and his desire to do his best for you. It's embarrassing, not only to him, but also to those who are watching and listening.

Finally, I'll say this. Criticize only if you can favorably influence *the Four P's of Production—Peak Performance for Peak Profits.*

And if you can't—don't!

Make Every Man Your Personal Trouble-Shooter

How'd you like to have a company where you had no problems—where no one ever made a mistake—where everything ran as smooth as silk every minute of the day? Would you like to have an outfit like that? Here's how you can:

Teach every man the Four P's of trouble-shooting: Prior Planning Prevents Problems. Show him how to use those Four P's in the Standard Operation Plan.

That would be too boring—too monotonous, you say? Having a company where you had no problems—where everything ran smoothly all day long? Too boring! Maybe so, but I'd like to carry your extra profits to the bank. That wouldn't get too boring; that wouldn't be monotonous at all!

Would you like to have a department so efficient that your boss would never have to send in efficiency experts or hire some outside business and management consultants to solve your problems for you? Would you look at that as a benefit worth having? Your boss would; I'm sure of that. And if you'd like to have the concrete benefit of working without having your boss breathing down the back of your neck all the time, here's how you can do just that.

Show each employee how to be an expert trouble-shooter. Teach him the problem-solving process.

What would you give to have an army of experts in your plant scouting around for profit leaks—prospecting for clues—nipping trouble in the bud even before it starts? And to add some frosting to your cake, you wouldn't have to pay them a penny extra to do this for you! You see, they're your regular employees already. You can get them to do this for you if . . .

You make each one your personal trouble – shooter.

All this is too idealistic, you say. I don't think so. Sure it's no snap; anything worthwhile never is. But if you don't shoot, you won't hit the target, and I don't care how old-fashioned or schoolboyish that might sound. It's still the truth.

Teach them to bring you answers – not questions.

"If you want to change every one of your subordinates into an expert trouble-shooter for you, get him to bring you some logical answers to his own problems right along with his questions," says Tom Hilton, executive vice-president of the Dennison Manufacturing Company.

"For example, just the other day I was walking through our plant, and I stopped to talk with one of our young supervisors. He told me about a problem he was having on one of his production lines.

"Well, he stopped right there; he'd gotten as far as the problem. At least, that's all he told me about. But that wasn't even half the distance. He hadn't even got started as far as I was concerned.

"What do you recommend?" I asked him. "You're the production supervisor. I want to know what you think we should do. If I don't agree with your answers, I'll say so. If it turns out to be a problem that you can't take care of, then I'll help you work it out. *But I want your ideas first; I want you to do the initial trouble-shooting for me.*

"Don't come to me with only problems," I told him. "Bring me ideas, plans, actions, alternatives. Bring me something I can sink my teeth into and chew on. Bring me some possible answers to your problem so I can help you make a proper decision.

"Get your people to do that, and you'll soon make every single employee in your plant your own personal trouble-shooter," Tom concludes. "And you need all the help you can get. It's a rough road when you try to travel it all alone."

Here's how you can recognize a real trouble-shooter.

The top-notch trouble-shooter has several prime qualities that the ordinary fellow doesn't have.

First of all, he's developed a sixth sense that helps him to anticipate the problem even before it happens. He can smell trouble brewing just as easily as you and I can smell a skunk!

And when he smells the slightest hint of trouble, he goes to work right then. He meets that trouble head on. He doesn't try to duck it or avoid it. He's developed the knack of coping with trouble and he's not afraid of it. Solving problems is the best way to develop your strength and to become an expert trouble-shooter yourself.

When he does run into problems, he doesn't run all over the place trying to stamp out the symptoms of the disease. He knows from past experience he can't get rid of any illness by treating the symptoms. He hunts for the source of the trouble so he can weed it out by its roots. When the cause is eliminated—the effect will disappear. The real trouble-shooter knows that so he gets rid of the cause; the ordinary employee treats the symptom.

Of course, the success of any good trouble-shooter depends upon his following the Four P's of trouble-shooting. He knows when he follows those rules, he won't have as much work to do; his troubles will be few and far between. And he knows it's a lot easier to prevent problems than it is to solve them, so he uses these Four P's of trouble-shooting—

Prior
Planning
Prevents
Problems.

All right; where do we stand right now? What's next? Well, by now you should have some idea of the benefits and advantages you can have when you make every man your personal trouble-shooter. You've seen how one top-level executive does it, and I've given you certain qualities a good trouble-shooter should have.

I've also said it's easier to prevent trouble than it is to cure it, so let's dig into that one first.

Prior Planning Prevents Problems.

If you use the Four P's of trouble-shooting, you can stop a lot of troubles before they ever start. You can shoot them down like clay pigeons on a skeet range. The clue is to keep your eyes on the bird and not let it get too high off the ground before you pull the trigger.

Use deliberate planning — violent execution.

The military uses the Four P's of trouble-shooting this way. *Deliberate planning and violent execution.* It's a good principle to use. We civilians use it in many things we do. Even your grandmother did. Remember the Thanksgiving and Christmas dinners she used to prepare for the family?

She planned the holiday feast for weeks ahead of time. She spent the final three or four days in elaborate preparation. The last eight to twelve hours were crucial for her. And twenty minutes after the table was spread, it looked for all the world like a disaster area! *Deliberate planning—violent execution!*

The proof of the pudding . . .

"Oh, you writers are all alike, Jim," Ken Copeland, of McDonald Aircraft in St. Louis and a good friend of mine, said to me. "You think up all sorts of fancy phrases and trick gimmicks, but how do I know they'll work for me?

"Just like that phrase of yours, 'Prior Planning Prevents Problems,'—the Four P's of trouble-shooting, as you call it. Sure sounds great. Rolls off the tongue real easy, but you show me in black and white how to do it—show me how it works—and I'll buy it!"

So I did. I gave Ken a skeleton outline (in writing, too!) for his own purposes and for his own operation so he could prove to himself that prior planning does prevent problems. He liked it. I think you will, too, so here it is—just as I gave it to Ken:

OPERATION PLAN

1. General Information.

a. *Competition.* Who, what, when, where, why, how. What is the general situation, the capabilities, and the indications of your competitive action? You must use an active intelligence system to keep up-to-date data for this subparagraph.

b. *Your own forces.* Exactly who and what do you have available to you to do the job? Can you expect or do you need outside assistance if it becomes necessary?

2. Mission.

State your exact mission that you expect to accomplish by issuing this operation plan. Be specific.

3. Execution.

a. In this first subparagraph, give your overall concept of how you are going to accomplish your assigned mission.

b. In each succeeding subparagraph, assign individual missions to each department, each division, or each section of your organization. Use one subparagraph for each individual element of your company.

c. In the last subparagraph, give your coordinating instructions that will apply to two or more elements of your organization.

4. Administration and Support.

Cover thoroughly, in as many subparagraphs as you need, the actions, the duties, and the assignments of your staff personnel, or of any element that will not actually participate in the accomplishment of your primary mission, but who will support your actual operational elements.

5. Special Instructions.

a. Here you should cover those miscellaneous items which are important to all elements of your company—including your staff and support people—but which are not necessarily a part of the execution outlined in Paragraph 3.

b. This subparagraph should contain the organizational policies of the president, the manager, the department head, or whoever the chief is who is issuing this operation plan. If the chief cannot be reached at his usual location during this operation, indicate here where he will be.

It works.

"When I first looked at this skeleton outline for your operation plan, I thought I was back in the army, Jim," says Bruce Miller, plant manager for one of the Scott paper mills. "I instinctively rebelled against it; automatic reaction, I guess. Never did like paperwork!

"But after the fiasco we'd had the year before with the auditors who tried to take our annual stock inventory, I thought I'd better try it. And it worked out fine. I was able to assign tasks and missions in a precise 1-2-3 fashion to the various departments and give them the extra help they needed to do the job. Everybody in the plant had a job to do; no one was left out—no one was forgotten.

"By following this detailed outline you gave me, I was able to come up with a complete operation plan for my inventory that was all inclusive. Nothing was left to chance. And as I said, it does work. When we took our annual inventory this time, it went off like a breeze. The auditors were done in less than 24 hours. We had to stop productive operations for less than 72 hours.

"Our planning phase took about three weeks; the actual physical count less than a day, and there were no foul ups anywhere; we had no problems. I even got a letter of appreciation from the front office for a job well done!"

And that's the key to it right there in Bruce's last paragraph. He didn't say it in so many words, but it's still there. *Deliberate prior planning—rapid execution.* Without that proper prior planning, there'd have been no rapid execution. Remember their previous annual inventory had been a fiasco!

It'll work for anything.

This skeleton outline of a plan will work for any possible operation you can dream up. You can use it for an annual inventory as Bruce did, or a proposed plant expansion study; working the bugs out of a new product; anything else you want to try it on.

Incidentally, when you don't have any information to put in a certain subparagraph, leave it blank. You don't have to fill up all the white space just to make it look as if you'd been busy. Suppose you were going to use it for an inventory. The chances are you wouldn't need to say anything about your competition in paragraph 1-a. But if you're talking about a new product—that paragraph could become mighty important!

Before it goes into effect, it's an operation plan. The moment you sign it, or when the date and time specified in it for execution is reached—it's no longer a plan—*it's an operation order.* So you can use it for two purposes at the same time: *planning and execution.*

And that's how I'd suggest that you make the Four P's of trouble-shooting—*prior planning prevents problems*—work for you.

Solve one problem every day.

"Try to solve one problem every day, and your place will soon be as bare of trouble as Mother Hubbard's cupboard," says Gus Swanson, who has his own meat packing plant in Iowa. "I give my men a goal to shoot for. I make them my personal trouble-shooters. Just like the traffic cop has a quota of tickets to write each day, I give my men a quota, too. They have to solve one problem a day—preferably one of their own!"

You can do the same thing yourself. Resolve each day to track down just one thing that isn't being done to your complete satisfaction. Then see that it's corrected.

Stick a trouble-shooting black book in your hip pocket.

Don't trust your memory; too many things can interfere before you get back to your office to write down what you saw. Jot things down as you see them. If you need some ideas for starting out, tackle a few like these:

1. Prolonged coffee breaks,

or clerical help gathered around one desk, an office machine, a water cooler, a pretty girl, etc.

2. Evidence of profit loss

through waste, careless handling of machinery and materials, a slipshod attitude toward company property, excessive rejection of the finished product by your quality control people.

3. Failure to meet realistic deadlines,

or some desks piled high with back paperwork and administration while others are bone bare. Is someone inefficient, or is there an improper distribution of the work load?

4. Increasing labor grievances

over minor matters. Constant trouble, disturbances, problems coming up in one department all the time.

5. Excessive overtime

by certain individuals on your office force night after night. Eager beaver, inefficient, or overmarried? Any person who can't get his normal work done in eight hours is either overloaded or underskilled, maybe even undersexed.

6. A deliberate slow-down of the work pace

can lead to the same amount of overtime for the same persons or the same department day after day in your production. If there isn't some variation of some sort, you have a definite problem.

7. Attitudes of your people

act as a special barometer for you to watch. Keep your eyes open for people walking around with short temper fuses. Listen for angry and heated telephone conversations—desk pounding. You can find trouble spots popping up here and there like the rash of measles. One man is bored with his job; another man couldn't care less whether school keeps or not; a third one hates his supervisor; another has personal problems that spill over into his work. All these are potential personnel problem areas for you to check on.

This is just a general sampling I've pulled at random from my own files to give you as examples. You'll be able to pinpoint specific ones in your own shop, I'm sure of that.

You must take the lead.

"In our business, our biggest headache is spoilage," says Lee Mercer, of United Fruit. "Any employee who can show us how to save an extra bunch of bananas, a sack of potatoes, or a basket of tomatoes is going to earn a bonus from us. But if you want him to be a good trouble-shooter for you, you've got to set the example for him to follow.

"You must step out and take the lead. Attack your problems aggressively to get rid of them. Use whatever means you have available. Shoot your troubles down while they're small; don't give them a chance to grow!"

To do that, you'll need to know how to make sound and timely decisions about your own business—your own employees. Whenever you make a decision, your reputation as a trouble-shooter will be at stake. You cannot hesitate; you cannot delay. Your employees will lose confidence in you if you do. So *make up your mind—reach a decision about your problem—issue an order to solve it.*

It's often a matter of timing.

Many of your business problems today have a timing factor in them. Put off your decision by a day or a week and it's too late; your competition has beaten you to the punch. So it becomes necessary for you to follow a definite and logical step-by-step procedure to solve your problems in an orderly and analytical manner. This is especially important when you're fighting an inflexible deadline so you'll not leave out some of the important details you might otherwise miss in the rush.

You must take careful aim first.

A young or inexperienced supervisor will often make the mistake of thinking he's losing valuable time by following a systematic step-by-step procedure when he uses the operation plan or the problem-solving process. He's like the tenderfoot in the old West who thought speed was the only essential in gun play. It wasn't. Important? Yes, but only after you'd taken careful aim at your opponent! Every successful gunfighter in the old West knew that; that's why he was alive and successful.

So don't make the mistake of pulling the trigger before you've taken a careful bead on your target. Remember the principle—deliberate planning; violent execution. You cannot reverse the procedure.

The problem–solving process

This is a sound and definite 1-2-3—by the numbers, do it—approach to solving problems and trouble-shooting. Use it, and you'll be guided to a logical and timely decision each time. There are three general steps to follow in this problem solving process: *Recognize the problem; make an estimate of the situation; take the appropriate action.*

1. Recognize the problem

In general, you could say you have some kind of trouble in your outfit whenever something happens that affects one or more of your four positive management indicators of leadership unfavorably.

However, to look at your problem only in terms of these four management indicators—*morale, esprit, discipline, and proficiency*—will not sufficiently identify and isolate your trouble for you.

There are many different human factors and a variety of conditions in your company that will influence each one of these positive management indicators of leadership. It's up to you to evaluate your own organization in the searchlight of each one of these indicators to fully isolate your trouble and to figure out its total impact on your operation.

For example, a wildcat strike can have its trouble roots in at least two of these broad areas (morale and discipline) and possibly a third (esprit). By the way, morale is usually thought of as being an individual proposition, while esprit is organizational and the sum total of these individual attitudes.

Once you've determined the general area and broad nature of your trouble, then you're ready to—

2. Make an estimate of the situation, by . . .

a. Determining the exact cause.

Before you ever try to solve any problem, to be a professional trouble-shooter, you must clearly define the exact nature of the problem. You must find out who is involved; what are the exact circumstances; when and where did it happen? The best way to do this is to run it through the gauntlet of those five questions words—
1. *Who,*
2. *What,*
3. *When,*
4. *Where,*
5. *Why (How).*

b. Determining the possible solutions.

After you've figured out the exact cause in Step 2-a by applying those five question words to your problem, then you're ready to look at the possible solutions. Don't throw out a solution just because it doesn't appear at first glance to be the right answer. Even if it won't solve today's problem—you might be able to use it tomorrow. So keep it in mind. And remember this, too. The more possible solutions you look at—the better your final solution is likely to be.

c. Weighing the possible solutions — one against the other.

When you've gathered up all the possible solutions, you're ready to compare them. However, before you do, weigh the advantages of one solution against its own disadvantages. *This is an important time-saver.*

Should the disadvantages outweigh the advantages to the point that the whole solution becomes impractical, don't compare it with the rest of the possible solutions. Set it aside for the next day's problems.

As a bit of guidance here, keep this thought in mind. Don't let your personal preferences, or worse, your personal prejudices, influence your decision when you're evaluating possible solutions others have suggested. For example, don't discard Smith's idea automatically just because he has halitosis, or Jones's suggestion because you're jealous that he has a beautiful and shapely, red-haired wife!

The only other point you need keep in mind which will allow you to reach a sensible and unbiased decision is this. Balance the scales of accomplishment of the mission and the welfare of your employees, and you'll never go far wrong.

d. Select the best solution.

A point well worth mentioning, for it's often overlooked, even by the most experienced executives, is this: The solution you pick might well be a combination of two of the suggested solutions you considered in Step 2-c. For instance, you might take half of Black's suggestion, half of White's, and come up with a *Gray solution* that fills the bill for you perfectly.

So use your imagination. Once you've got your thinking in the groove on this, don't be afraid to swing out of the pattern once in a while. It's not so cut and dried that you can't improve it for yourself.

3. Take the appropriate action.

Here, now, you simply put the solution you've chosen—the decision you've made—into immediate effect. Use those leadership techniques that happen to fit your particular personality and way of doing things. Don't hesitate and waver with indecision now. Your hard work is finished. So take the appropriate action; issue the necessary order, and then—

Supervise the execution of your order.

The best trouble-shooter in the world will fall flat on his face unless he sees that his order is carried out. All that corrective action won't be worth a nickel to you if you don't follow up and supervise. You can't be satisfied with just starting the corrective action; you've got to keep the ball rolling.

Your ultimate success will usually depend upon your own persistence and your willingness to supervise and to check the results of your efforts. I can't stress this point too much. One of the most distinguishing features of a superior trouble-shooter, and one that separates him from the mediocre ones, is his ability to vigorously carry out and supervise an effective course of corrective action.

So use this problem-solving process; teach it to your subordinates and get them to use it, too. The more you practice this art of solving problems, the more often you'll be able to arrive at the right decision the first time out. Soon you'll be able to cut your troubles off at the roots before they have a chance to grow. When you reach that point, you can call yourself a real trouble-shooter!

Give your subordinates full responsibility for solving their own problems.

Teach a man the problem-solving process, and then give him the responsibility for solving his own problems. Let him do his own trouble-shooting. You'll both enjoy your work more when you do. When you give your employee the responsibility for doing a job, then you must also give him the authority to make on-the-spot decisions about that job.

"If you don't delegate the authority to your employees to carry out the responsibilities you've given them, if you won't let them do their own trouble-shooting, then you've made a mistake by picking the wrong people for their jobs in the beginning," says Oscar Benjamin of Inland Steel.

"Or could be you're a neurotic yourself. Not too many production workers visit a psychiatrist, but management people keep his appointment book full. Anyway, if you delegate responsibility, but not authority, you're about like the split personality who likes sex, but hates women!

"You shouldn't have to waste time in long conferences making decisions because your own staff has failed to shoulder their full responsibilities. Maybe it's your fault; maybe you didn't give them the authority they need to make their own decisions. If you've tied their hands so they can't do any of your trouble-shooting for you, you'd better call a special staff meeting right now and change your policies!"

Mr. Benjamin is so right. Delegating responsibility but not the authority makes for a situation where you want to accept the credit, but you don't want any part of the blame. Far too many supervisors—even high level executives—operate that way, unfortunately.

You can't take credit for everything a subordinate does that's right if you try to pass him the buck when something goes wrong. When you do that, you're like the father at the football game who cries, "That's *my* son!" when his boy makes the winning touchdown, but turns to his wife with the comment, "Look at what *your* son just did!" when his fumble is recovered by the opposing team.

And now in recap . . .

Inspire every man to be your personal trouble-shooter and you can relax and go fishing, or take a nap from two to four. When he uses the problem-solving process, your problems will become a thing of the past. And when an employee feels that he's your personal trouble-shooter, he'll want to work that much harder for you. After all, he's your personal envoy—your special representative! With this sense of added responsibility, he'll start thinking up new ways of doing things—he'll look for short cuts to reduce costs and increase profits.

When he starts bringing you answers instead of questions, he'll be developing his own ideas. That'll be to your benefit, too. I'll tell you how you can get him to do that in the next chapter.

Successful Ideas Are 2% Inspiration —
98% Perspiration

Today we have transistors in our radios, our television sets, and our hi-fi systems to replace the old-fashioned vacuum tube. Why? Well, transistors do not produce heat. They are virtually trouble free, and they last indefinitely. But that doesn't really tell why at all, does it? *Then why?*

Because someone had a better idea!

Every invention, from the first crude wheel to the intricate and highly sophisticated control system of a manned space rocket, had its beginning in the dark caverns of the mind. A tiny seed of thought was planted in a brain furrow; it was plowed under by the conscious mind and allowed to germinate for a while. Then it was watered and fertilized by the subconscious, and finally—it bore good fruit. And you and I both benefited because—

Someone had a better idea!

Almost every major innovation you can name came into existence because a persistent man with an idea wouldn't give up. That's why I say a successful idea is only 2 percent inspiration and 98 percent perspiration. Remember Thomas Edison? Joseph Pirone?

People who pioneer with their minds almost always go through bitter disappointments before they succeed. What separates the men from the boys here is an extra gallon of sweat; a stubborn refusal to quit until they are proven to be conclusively wrong. And even then . . . .

I could go on and on reciting one example after another to show you how the ideas of man have benefited us in the past 50 years. But I don't need to; look around your own home—you can find a dozen examples yourself. I'll sum it up for you this way. I think Ford's motto could serve as the hallmark of our highly technological and scientific era: *Ford has a better idea!*

Money-making ideas are hard to come by.

Let's not kid ourselves. Good, usable, labor-saving and profit-making ideas are hard to come by. Not that people don't have good ideas; they do, but they don't develop them. That's why I said, in effect, that creative ability is 2 percent inspiration and 98 percent perspiration. And in spite of all the fancy deodorants we have, the average man just doesn't like to sweat.

"I just had the most brilliant idea!" Jack Jones exclaims. His face glows with enthusiasm; his eyes sparkle with imagination. "But it would take . . . and then there'd be . . . and he wouldn't . . . and I couldn't . . . . Forget it. It wasn't such a good idea after all!"

And so a fresh idea dies before it was even decently born. Jack had the 2 percent inspiration, all right. He just didn't have the 98 percent perspiration it takes to develop his momentary spark of creative genius.

Millions of dollars are lost every year because valuable ideas stay locked up in the minds of their owners. And not only is money lost, but also a better way of doing things.

Right there I've given you the two big benefits of cultivating the ideas of your employees—your advantages of getting them to think for you.

MORE MONEY AND A BETTER WAY OF DOING THINGS

You might as well get your share of both of them; if you don't, someone else will!

Money — money — and more money!

Certain names have become historically synonymous with money in these United States. There are hundreds more than I'll mention here, and a lot more recent ones, too. (You can still make a million dollars in spite of taxes; it just takes a little longer.) Most people recognize immediately such names as Ford, Firestone, Schwab, Carnegie, Morgan, Chrysler, Rockefeller.

Since most people associate these names with huge financial undertakings, massive corporations, huge conference tables in thick carpeted board rooms, few could imagine that the famous John D. Rockefeller was the central figure in this short scene. As big and important as he was, Mr. Rockefeller knew that *the continuing growth of his huge personal fortune depended mainly upon the new ideas of his employees.* That's why I'm telling it to you.

One day Mr. Rockefeller stopped by the desk of a junior executive who had recently joined his firm. That young man was burning with energy. He read papers at a furious pace; he shifted a piece of business correspondence from his in-basket to his out-basket every fifteen seconds.

Mr. Rockefeller watched him in silence for a few minutes. Then he put a hand on the young man's shoulder and said gently, "You mustn't work so hard!"

The young junior executive was amazed at Mr. Rockefeller's words. He had thought that the best way to impress Mr. Rockefeller was to show him how busy he was. But he was completely wrong; this wasn't Mr. Rockefeller's idea of how a young up-and-coming junior executive should work at all.

"You should teach your secretary how to do all that paperwork. That's what she's getting paid for," said Mr. Rockefeller. "Then you can put your feet up on your desk and think up some new ways to help Standard Oil make more money! That's what you're getting paid for."

Think up some new ways to make more money.

I can't think of a better reason to have fresh, new ideas; can you? Unless it's a better way of doing things, and that usually ends up making more money for you, too.

A better way of doing things.

Had there not been a young construction engineer named Freeman, the Grand Coulee Dam might never have become a reality. For in building it, the engineers ran up against a seemingly impossible problem. They reached a point where their normal construction methods would not work because of deep deposits of constantly shifting sand and mud. Tons of it poured into newly excavated areas; it ripped out pilings and scaffolding. All kinds of engineering devices and tricks were tried. No results. For a while, it looked hopeless. There seemed to be no possible answer to their dilemma. Some of the best engineering minds in the business were almost ready to give up the vast project.

Then one of the young engineers, Fred Freeman, had an inspired idea. "We can drive pipes down through all that sand and mud," he said. "Then we can circulate a refrigerant through them, and freeze the whole muddy mess solid as a rock! Once it's frozen, we won't have to worry about it coming down on top of us while we work."

They tried Fred's idea. In a short time, the unmanageable and shifting wet sands and mud had been frozen into a huge solid block. They could have built a skyscraper on it had they wanted to. So the Grand Coulee Dam came into existence and millions of people in the Pacific Northwest have benefited because one man, Fred Freeman, figured out *a better way of doing things.*

If you think more money and a better way of doing things are worthwhile benefits to you, then read on, my friend, read on. Here's how you can do it.

Coax a new idea into existence.

Ask a man for his counsel, his help, and his advice.

Ask an employee for his help and his advice on a particular matter—tell him you need his valuable assistance in solving a problem and you'll do two important things. First of all, you'll give him a feeling of importance; you'll build up his self-confidence.

Secondly, he'll be anxious to work harder for you and help you as a result of your confidence in him.

These two points—a feeling of importance and self-confidence, and the desire to work harder for you and help you—are a must if you want a man to exercise his brain muscles for you. Establish them as a firm foundation if you want this man to think up some money-making and labor-saving ideas for you.

He could have a lot of good thoughts that'll never bubble up to the top if you don't ask for his help. You must establish the creative climate for him. By showing him you have faith in his abilities to produce, you'll give him that self-confidence he needs. He has to feel confident in his own abilities before he can produce positive money-making ideas for you. It's up to you to give him that feeling.

Establish the creative climate.

If you could coax a fish to jump out of the water into your frying pan, you'd never have to figure out a better way to catch a fish, would you? There'd be no reason to. So the most important initial incentive in producing a new idea is pressure, a requirement, a need, an urgency for getting the job done. Hunger produced the bow and arrow. Within reason, pressure of deadlines and time limits helps to bring out a man's best creative powers.

Having seen two wars, one in Europe—the other in Korea, and neither one further back than an infantry battalion headquarters, I most definitely do not advocate war as a way of settling an argument. It accomplishes nothing. But medicine, for example, has made tremendous strides, because of the heavy pressures placed upon it to find answers, and to find them quickly.

"Medicine today has advanced much further than it would have by the year two thousand," says Dr. Rodney Charles, professor of internal medicine at George Washington University's famed Medical School in St. Louis. "And all because of war. We had no time to spend in leisurely research. We needed everything yesterday!"

Unless this sense of urgency exists, your employees will not come up with new ideas. They'll not try to figure out a better way of doing things unless there's a valid reason for them to do so. Thet's why it's so important that you insist that *you need their help!* I'm going to give you eight steps to follow that will help you establish this creative climate so new ideas will come your way.

1. Tell a man what you want.

Be specific. What kind of an idea do you need? Give your employee some sort of a target to draw a bead on. Exactly what is your problem? What do you want to improve? Unless you can answer this for him concretely—you have no goal for him at all. Thinking only in general terms isn't enough; his creative instincts will remain asleep. It's like thinking— *I'd like to be rich.* That isn't enough; the question is: *How?*

2. Give him all the facts.

Gather up all the pertinent information and useful data you can to give him a push in the right direction. Let him know the unsuccessful methods that you've already tried; let him know what doesn't work. Don't let him waste his time going up dead ends and blind alleys. Why should he have to spin his wheels aimlessly? Throwing out useless methods is definite progress.

3. Let him try the obvious first.

Amazingly, he may not have to go any further to find the idea you're looking for. Then why couldn't you find it? For the same reason that it's easier for you to spot mistakes in someone else's department or someone else's company. You're too close to the problem.

4. Turn him on.

Get him to use his imagination. When a man is trying to think up new ideas, he has to throw all logic and caution and reason out the window. He must tackle the problem from every angle whether it makes sense or not.

5. Bear down.

Get him to concentrate on his task; get him to think about it intensely. Tell him to stick to it until he comes up with a new idea. Never let him give up until he reaches his own tolerance combustion point.

6. Tell him to forget it.

When he's done all that he can do—let him forget it for a while. He's done his part. He's planted the creative seed. Now let the subconscious harvest the crop.

7. Be prepared for the answer.

No one knows how long that subconscious mind will simmer away. Sooner or later, though, the idea—the answer he's been waiting for—will bubble up to the top. And when it does, it usually surfaces with the speed of a hooked salmon. So he must be ready for it, no matter whether he's shaving, eating, driving the car, working, or watching television.

He must be ready to write it down the moment the message comes through. It will never come again as clearly as the first time. In fact, in most cases, it never will come again. The subconscious mind is very stubborn. It figures once is enough. Take it or leave it!

8. Act on it.

Test the idea. Put it to work. Try it out. You may have to modify it to make it work. Eventually, you might even have to discard it, but you'll save enough ideas to make the whole system worth all the effort.

"You must take special care to be ready for the answer,"

says Ted Martin, vice-president in charge of advertising for Continental Can. "I am especially watchful for that moment of sudden insight. There's no rhyme or reason as to how or when the answer will come to you. It can come through the most unlikely channel at the most improbable time. The answer can leap from a printed page or emerge from a blank wall. I've had it come to me at the most inopportune moments when I've been driving down the turnpike at 75 miles an hour, for instance. Or in the shower, which is even more inconvenient!"

Write it down!

I know what Ted is driving at. He needs to get the idea written down before it gets away from him. To be able to catch that sudden impulse, I always carry half a dozen 3" by 5" cards and a pencil in my shirt pocket. In the car, I keep my portable tape recorder handy. In the nightstand are some 5" by 8" cards and another pencil. It's harder for me to write legibly when I awake from a sound sleep with an idea. That bigger card allows for more scrawling.

When the idea comes to you, no matter how crazy it seems at the time, write down enough of it so it'll be as clear and understandable a month or a year later as it is at that moment. I didn't always do that. Today, I have some cards in my files that have only one or two words written on them. I was so sure I'd never forget my code when I wrote the message down, but I've had some of those cards for nearly five years now, and I still don't know what they mean!

Give a courteous hearing to his ideas.

"I don't care how fantastic or how ridiculous a man's idea might sound to you at the moment, hear him out," says Paul Nolan, one of the top engineers for Fairbanks-Morse of Canada.

"Several years ago we took a contract to run electricity to Fort MacKenzie, a trading outpost in northern Saskatchewan. We were able to get the powerhouse built; we had the generators and the engines installed, and we had all seventy houses and the three stores wired up.

"We had less than a mile of high line to string when we got caught with an early winter. Temperatures dropped to fifty below and we had no way to set up the poles for that final stretch of line. Unless we got that line in by the first of December, we'd lose a big chunk of money, but no one could figure out how to dig holes in ground that was frozen more than four feet deep! And you can't set a pole in the ground without a hole; nor can you string a line without a pole!

"Then one of our boys came forward with an idea. 'Blow out holes with dynamite,' he said. 'Fill the holes with water and set the poles in the water. The water will freeze to ice, and it'll hold the poles solid as a rock until the spring thaw comes. Then we can set 'em up proper with dirt.'

"It worked. We had a lot of other bugs to work out, like getting the dynamite into the ground to blow the hole, but we solved each problem as we went along. For example, the dynamite hole was made by pounding a steel rod into the ground with a sledge hammer. But first we had to heat the rod red hot to get it into the frozen ground! And we had to heat it forty to fifty times for each dynamite hole, but we did it. We used a portable forge that we dragged along from one hole to the next.

"We blew nearly eighty holes in the ground that looked like giant coffee cups. We carried the water from the river with bobsleds using two 100-gallon drums with faucets welded on them. We had to thaw out the faucets each time with a blow torch to get the water out of the barrels and into the holes for the uprights.

"But we got the job done. And we did it by using a suggestion that sounded completely idiotic when we first heard it!"

If you go to all the effort of setting up the right creative climate to coax some new ideas into existence, it wouldn't make any sense for you to turn a deaf ear to a man's suggestions. As Paul Nolan just said, the idea sounded idiotic when he first heard it, but it worked!

Many ideas may sound fantastic to you, too, but it's important that you do not act scornful or impatient. There's no surer way to discourage your employee's original thinking than to make fun of him or to ridicule one of his ideas. His next idea could well be the one you really need, so you'd better make sure that it's easy to come by.

Are you guilty of turning off fresh ideas?

Do you stop the ideas of your employees cold with your negative attitude? If you use any of the following comments, I can guarantee you're an idea stopper. You've got the suggestions of your employees all bottled up, and you're the cork!

We have other much more important things to do.

Your timing isn't just right.

I don't think they'd go for that idea.

Surely you don't mean *that* again?

Who else has tried it?

Oh come now, is it really that big a problem?

Let me think about that for a while; I'll let you know.

No, it won't work; we've tried it before.
It's not for us.
We've always done it this way.
People won't accept it.
Everybody's doing it this way now.
No one else is doing it that way.
No, it's impractical.
I'll think it over.
We don't have time to try it out.
It's way too old.
It's far too new.
It's too . . . .
So don't be an idea stopper; give a courteous hearing to a man's ideas. You can if you'll learn—

How to judge an idea.

To judge the value of a new idea, you have to run it through at least four questions before you make the decision of whether to accept it or reject it.

1. Does the idea yield the desired results?

Does it give you what you're really looking for? Is it a better way of doing things? Will it actually increase your profits? Will it save you time in a particular phase of your activity? This is an important one to check, for any ideas that will save you time will usually make you more money. If the idea won't do any of these things for you, the chances are it's not the answer you're looking for. But don't give up; have your employee keep working to improve his idea.

2. Is his idea a real improvement over your present system?

Some ideas that your employees come up with are impractical to put into operation, not because they don't work, but because nothing really important is gained. Suppose one of your men figured out a lever that would replace a button on a certain piece of machinery, the question is not so much whether it will work or not, but whether it's *a better way of doing things.* That's the real test of the idea.

3. Does it cost too much?

It doesn't make good economic sense to spend a thousand dollars to install some apparatus that'll save you 93 cents a week, for example, especially if the life expectancy of the machinery you're improving is only five more years. Your recovery rate in dollars and cents has to be realistic. Even it you can see where the cost can be recovered in a reasonable length of time, keep in mind that another new idea six months later could make this one old-fashioned. We're advancing so fast in technical and scientific know-how today that the long range value of a product is often less predictable than the length of your wife's dress.

4. Is it well-timed?

This ties in closely with number three. Some youngsters today have never seen an old-fashioned butter churn like Grandma used to have in the kitchen. And with the continual climb of food costs, it could seem like a good invention, especially if you came up with an electric one. However, the inconvenience of churning butter at home makes it about as timely as an improved buggy whip. Seriously though, every idea, to be worthwhile, must be usable in the time frame in which it's to be implemented.

Tell the originator of an idea what action you took — and why.

Do this, and he'll study other problems for you and make suggestions on ways to solve them. If his idea is accepted, he'll be encouraged by seeing the results of his thinking put into action. If his idea is not adopted, he'll be able to accept that fact more readily and with a fuller understanding if you show him why you couldn't use it. When he knows why his idea was not practical and why it couldn't be used, he'll be able to analyze the next problem you hand him to work on more clearly.

"Don't let an employee get the feeling his ideas are being burned in the trash barrel," says Tom Willard of the Cooper Tire and Rubber Company. "That's why our company won't use a suggestion box; it's too impersonal. And we don't use a form rejection slip either. We let every man who submits a suggestion know exactly what happens to it, and why. He gets plenty of opportunity to rebut our rebuttal."

Let people carry out their own ideas.

A man will work more enthusiastically on his own idea than he will on someone else's. Nine times out of ten, his suggestion is about his own department or his own line of work, anyway.

Once in a while, it could happen that equally good suggestions on a particular problem will come from two people at the same time, especially if you've made a plant-wide appeal for help. When this happens, one person will be more directly involved in the problem than the other one.

In such cases, it would be wise to choose the recommendation submitted by the man who'll eventually be working on it. He'll have a personal stake in proving that his own idea is a workable one. Just be sure all your employees know your policy; don't make the rules of the game as you go along. Make them before you blow the starting whistle.

Your employees will go along with you if you have a fair system. The law of averages will balance everything out for them.

Build up your men's sense of value of their work.

Ask a man for suggestions about how to improve the work methods on his own job, and you'll make that job more important to him. Most people, myself included, need to think that what they do is important. This is even more noticeable today than previously, for a variety of reasons. First of all, we're in a scientific age—the age of techno-mania—technicians are everywhere.

Because of computers, we've come to think of people as numbers—not names. But we're not numbers and we're not sheep and we're not cattle. We're people, and we like to be treated that way. So the average man won't really start clicking in his job until he feels that he's essential. Asking a man for his own ideas about his job will make that job more important to him, and you'll be more important to him, too.

To summarize . . . .

Just a few points now to emphasize what I've covered in this chapter. Remember the benefits you can win from your men's ideas—*money and a better way of doing things*. And to get these two big benefits, you must—

1. Coax new ideas into existence by asking your men for their help and their advice.
2. Establish the creative climate by
    a. Telling a man what you want.
    b. Giving him all the facts bearing on the problem.
    c. Letting him try the obvious first.
    d. Getting him to use his imagination.
    e. Having him think about the problem intensely.
    f. Letting him forget it for a while.
    g. Watching for the answer.
    h. Trying it out.
3. Give a courteous hearing to his ideas.
4. Tell him what action you took—and why.
5. Let him carry out his own ideas.
6. Build up his own sense of value of his work.

So give it a whirl, will you? It's worth it!

THE 11TH SECRET

Find the Right Button,

and then —

Punch It!

Let me ask you a personal question. If your boss asked you to do something that was a bit out of the ordinary, routine run of things, what would your first reaction be? Come now, don't be bashful. I know it makes you sound selfish, but it's the truth, isn't it? You still don't want to commit yourself?

All right, I'll tell you. Oh, you might not want to come right out and say this to your boss point-blank, but I know you're going to be thinking—

What's in it for me?

You don't think so? I'll bet you the time-honored dollar to a doughnut I'm right. Here's why:

Look at a group picture you know you were in. A football team, baseball team, family group, company picnic. Where do your eyes go first? *To yourself!*

Whenever you have a dream, who's the central character—the hero? *You are!*

Open a newspaper and turn to the stock market quotations. What's your main concern? *The value of your own stock.*

Why? You're self-centered; that's why. I'm not criticizing you—I'm merely stating a simple fact. I'm self-centered, too; we all are. That's nature's way of perpetuating the species; it's a natural law of self-preservation.

Oh, from time to time, especially in an emergency, some of us can overcome this human trait of selfishness and sacrifice our own interests for others. But it has to be a real crisis and not many of us make the grade. That's why Congressional Medals of Honor and Distinguished Service Medals are often awarded posthumously, and why there are so few of them. They definitely are not cheaper by the dozen! The price is exceedingly high.

We respond to those things that help us.

Most of us respond best to those things that affect our comfort and happiness, our safety and bank accounts. To me—the earth revolves around me; I am the central point. To you—the earth revolves around you; you are the central point.

What am I driving at? Simply this. I'm trying to show you that if you want to find the right button on your employee, and then punch it to turn him on—you must realize *he's self-centered, too. His world revolves around him; he is his own central point.*

In order to find the right push button, you've got to find out whether his primary circuit is wired for love, gain, duty, pride, self-indulgence, or what have you. If you punch the wrong button, he won't start.

Take advantage of this knowledge of him in your orders, your requests, your suggestions. Phrase your message in terms that *spell out to your employee what's in it for him.* Remember, that'll always be the uppermost question in his mind, even if it remains unspoken.

Beat him to the punch.

Answer his question before he asks it. Tell him what's in it for him. Then he'll respond. A young lieutenant understood that secret well. We were walking along the streets of Monterey, the city just outside of Fort Ord, California. It was a Saturday afternoon; the streets were crowded with soldiers.

Each one we met saluted him smartly. "I don't understand it," I said. "Soldiers are notoriously lax about saluting second lieutenants, and yet—every one we've met has given you a highball! And they're off-duty, too!"

"You haven't been watching, Jim," Tom said with a grin. "They don't have much choice. I've been saluting them first!"

That was his secret: *beating them to the punch.* You can do the same. Tell your employee what's in it for him. Don't expect him to accept your idea for *what it is* or *what it'll do for you.* He won't! But he will accept your suggestion when he knows *what it'll do for him!* Now it's really your turn to ask,

"What's in it for me?"

Let me give you a couple of examples to illustrate. I think you can see immediately the benefits you'd gain. Then I'll give you a fast summary of your advantages when you find a man's right button—and punch it.

You can work the suggestion in all directions, up or down, even sideways. You can aim it down at your employees, up at your boss, and laterally at your co-workers.

For instance, let's go up.

Want your boss to put his stamp of approval on a new piece of machinery you want installed on your production line? Then don't describe the operation of some new-fangled gadget. Don't tell him about its slick paint job or its fancy buttons and levers. Those are features.

Sell your boss the same way that Kenmore salesman down at Sears sold your wife her new automatic washer. *Sell your boss benefits; tell him how it will help him!* Show him how that new machine will eliminate injuries, get rid of lost production time, boost morale, give him a better quality product, and put more money in his pocket. *Now you're really punching his button!*

Now let's go down.

Want a stubborn employee to use his safety equipment? Don't tell him how much an injured employee is going to cost your company. When you do that, you're talking about your benefits—not his. Talk to him in his language. Tell him about the serious injuries that could cause the loss of a foot, a hand, or an eye—how he could be crippled for life—if he continues with his careless attitude.

To summarize, then, when you find an employee's right button and punch it, you'll benefit by—

1. *Getting things done right the first time* for your men can see what's in it for them when they do.

2. *Saving time and money* by avoiding errors, misunderstanding, and needless backtracking. And that means *extra profits to you!*

3. *Getting complete cooperation* from your employees when you show them how your ideas will benefit them.

And when you punch your boss's right button, you can benefit by—

   1. *Getting a promotion,*

    2. *A bonus,*

     3. *A raise.*

And all this without polishing the apple, either! To punch his button, all you have to do is *Find out what he needs—and help him get it!*

I. FIND HIS BUTTON.

Find out what a man needs — and help him get it!

This is the most important secret of salesmanship. But it's so obvious, 95 percent of all salesmen miss it. That's why only 5 percent become top-notch salesmen. It's also the biggest factor in the success of any business, any company or corporation—an executive, manager, foreman or supervisor.

The company that attempts to operate without finding out what the customer wants and helping him get it is foredoomed to failure. The manager or the business executive who doesn't do that for his employees as well as his customers is not destined to be a manager for long.

Russell Conwell, in his wonderful little book, *Acres of Diamonds,* tells about the time his father left him in charge of his country store. He had not yet learned this great secret of salesmanship. He learned it only after he became a minister! Here's what he said, in effect:

"A man came into the store and said to me, 'Do you have jackknives?' 'No, we don't!' I said, and off I went, whistling to myself. I didn't care about what that man wanted. I had more important things to do!

"Then a second man came in and asked me the same thing. I gave him the same answer. And yet a third man came in wanting a jackknife, and I said, 'No, we don't carry jackknives. You're the third person this morning who's wanted one. Do you think we run a big store like this just to sell such a little thing as a jackknife? You'll have to get it somewhere else. We don't carry such small items!'

"Thank heavens, my father did not leave me in charge of his store very often. Had he done so I'm afraid he'd have soon lost his entire business!"

Finding out what a man wants—and helping him get it—is a philosophy to live by.

Frank Bettger, one of the greatest salesmen America has ever known, says this in his book, *How I Raised Myself from Failure to Success in Selling,* published by Prentice-Hall, Inc., Englewood Cliffs, New Jersey.

"The most important secret of salesmanship is to find out what the other fellow wants. Then help him find the best way to get it. This is the one big secret of selling anything. It's something more than a sales technique, too. It's a law.

"When you show a man what he wants, he'll move heaven and earth to get it. This universal law is of such paramount importance that it takes precedence over all other laws of human relations. It always has been, and always will be the most important. It looms up as Rule Number One over all other rules in civilization. *It's a philosophy to live by!*"

The Six Prime Movers.

Your job is to find out which prime mover will incite each employee to his maximum; which one will cause him to do what you want him to do; which one will most stir him to the point where the motive becomes stronger than his inertia.

Every human being has six prime interests. I've mentioned these before, away back in the beginning of the book. To refresh your memory, they are *love, gain, duty, pride, self-indulgence, and self-preservation.*

Some of you might think I'm repeating myself, and perhaps I am, but only in a way. The last time we approached this, we came at it from the north side; this time we're attacking it from the south side. Besides, the famous memory expert, Dr. Bruno Furst, says that it takes *68 repetitions* to learn a simple thing in one day, and *504 repetitions* if it's at all complicated! I haven't even begun to approach those figures.

Speaking of repetition, I'm reminded of my nephew, Timothy Kelly. (His father was that Marine!) Before his first day of school rolled around, his mother, Beulah, sensibly made every possible effort to indoctrinate her son. She talked about school so enthusiastically that he was anxious for that first day to come. Off he went, wearing his new clothes, happy and cheerful.

The next morning when he came to the breakfast table, he had on his old sneakers, some patched jeans, and a tattered shirt.

"Timmy, why didn't you put on your school clothes?" his mother asked. "You'll have to change right after breakfast."

"School!" said Tim, looking at his mother in astonishment. "Again? I thought we got rid of that yesterday!"

So if you feel it's repetitious, bear with me. It really isn't. Anyway, this business of learning the secrets of supervision is a lot like sex in some ways. It's fun to keep trying.

Punch every button you can.

Many times these six prime movers of a man are all mixed up together. Then it's hard to tell which one represents a man's strongest emotion. Just for instance, you might want a new car, solely because of a feeling of pride and keeping up with the Joneses. Unless you have so much money you can write a check without looking at your bank balance, you'll seldom buy a new car on the motive of pride alone. There has to be more.

The more motives you can appeal to, the more buttons you can punch. The more buttons you punch—the greater your chances of success. However, it's important that you distinguish between a motive that makes him *want to do,* what you desire, and one that *forces him to do it.*

The six basic fears.

Some salesmen and some supervisors use a man's basic fears to control him. These six basic fears are—
  1. *Poverty.*
    2. *Criticism.*
      3. *Ill health.*
        4. *Loss of love or respect.*
          5. *Old age.*
            6. *Death.*
These negative prime movers of a man can be counterbalanced by the positive prime movers. For example, the fear of criticism can be eliminated by appealing to a man's sense of pride. I would far rather appeal to a man's positive prime movers. When you do, you're appealing to a motive that will make him *want to do* what you want him to do rather than *forcing him to do it* because of fear.

When you appeal to one of the negative prime movers, *you are forcing him.* He'll not do it willingly. For instance, you can arouse a man's basic fear of poverty by threatening to fire him if his job performance doesn't improve. But even if he does improve his workmanship, you'll have lost his loyalty and his trust.

Always use the positive prime movers to punch the right button; you're on much safer ground when you do.

Love is always the strongest motive.

Love of a wife, a sweetheart, a child, will cause a man to steal for them. You can see how people every day sacrifice everything they have for love. A man who will sacrifice his own life on the battlefield to save his comrades has a love for mankind that goes beyond the understanding of most of us.

Love is one of the most difficult motives to work effectively without being misunderstood. Because it's so universal, it's been harped on by some profiteers so much that you'll have to be exceptionally careful in its use. You must disguise it to make it work effectively with your employees.

Try this new approach.

I'd like to suggest this new approach. Jesus said the second great commandment was to *love thy neighbor as thyself.* But that commandment is so hard for the average man to understand and to put into practice, he often gives up without even trying.

Jesus actively expressed his love for mankind by helping them—healing the sick, feeding the hungry, making people happy. So I'd suggest that you forget about love in its usual connotation, and spell it a new way. Spell love *H-E-L-P.* Then practice that by using it in your own shop with your own employees. Just *help him;* let the philosophers worry about how you should love him.

Gain is an easy motive to plug.

Show a man how to pick up some extra dollars in his pay envelope. He'll work his head off for you. You'll be doing both of yourselves a favor. Again, easy does it, for the idea of gain has been worked to death, but most of us are ambitious, and money speaks a language we all understand.

Pride strikes at the very core of a man.

Some of you might think the Green Bay Packers have always been a top football team. Not so! In 1956 the Packers lost twice as many games as they won. In 1957 they lost three times as many. In 1958, out of twelve games—*they lost ten!*

It's true that pro football is a sport, but it's also big business. A losing team doesn't stick around long.

And then came—you know who—*Vince Lombardi!*

Most of you think he's a superman, a coach with a magic touch, and so he is. He knows how to appeal to a man's positive motives—his basic prime movers! He built a winning team with the same men who'd made up the losing team before—including Bart Starr!

He appealed to a man's sense of pride and duty when he said, "The harder a man works, the harder it is to surrender." He coined slogan after slogan for his team to follow, including this prize winning statement. *"Pride is what causes a winning team's performance."*

If you like football, you know Mr. Lombardi's record. He came to Green Bay in 1959. They've been winning ever since. You may not know many other coaches' names in professional football, but I'll bet you know Mr. Green Bay Packer—Mr. Football himself—Vince Lombardi!

Show a man what it will do for him.

I don't think I need to cover each motive individually here. You know what makes a man tick if you'll face yourself honestly in the mirror and tell yourself the truth. You know what you want; you're a human being. Your employees are also human beings so you ought to be able to figure out what they want, too.

Just treat each one as an individual. Don't make any mass assumptions. We all might like music, but not everyone appreciates opera. Some people like fish; others wouldn't touch it. Recognize the fact we all have individual tastes. That's why you must find out what each person wants *most of all* so you can punch the right button.

To sum it up, arousing the *right motive* in a man, punching the right button, boils down to getting him to *want to do* what you want him to do by showing him *what it will do for him!*

II. PUNCH IT!

Supplying that impulse.

Watch the crowd sometimes at a carnival sideshow. At just the right moment in the barker's pitch, his assistants in the crowd start edging toward the ticket window. *And you move forward automatically without even realizing it!*

When you give an order or a suggestion to one of your employees, or whenever you tell your boss your new money-making idea, you'll also face that same critical moment. *You have to get the crowd moving.* Your prospect is almost convinced. Now you've got to cinch it.

You have his *attention.* You've aroused his *interest.* You've stimulated his *desire;* now you want him to take that last step—*action.* That, incidentally, is the AIDA formula—attention, interest, desire, action.

But he's not quite ready to take the plunge. Caution or inertia is holding him back. The third step—*desire*—is pushing him on. He's hesitating—teetering on the brink. But he hates to take that final step—*action*—for it forces him to make a decision.

Urge him too much—he'll draw back. No action. Urge him too little—same thing. No action. What to do?

Give him a push without seeming to do so.

Be that sideshow barker at the carnival. Supply the impulse to make it easier for him to go forward than to stand still or draw back. How?

You already know which button you're going to push—which motive is strongest with this individual. Now just look for some *easy minor point* he can say *"Yes"* to. That'll keep him headed toward your ticket window.

Take a tip from the big-ticket professional salesman.

Sears Roebuck says, "Satisfaction guaranteed or your money back. No questions. No money down. Try it for 30 days at our expense; if you don't like it—bring it back."

That's salesmanship. The customer takes no risks. Even the fellow selling an overcoat in the men's clothing department uses the same line.

"Don't decide now," he says. "Plenty of time for that later. We've got that coat in your exact size. Fits you perfectly. Don't take it off—wear it home! Try it for 30 days. Wear it around town and compare it with anything else you can find. Then decide whether you want to keep it or not. If you decide you don't like it—won't cost you a penny. We'll just slip it on your SRC account. Nope, doesn't mean a thing—merely a formality to make it easy for the stockroom to keep track of stuff. Comes off your account as easily as it goes on."

See how easy that salesman makes it for the buyer? Nothing to worry about. No major decision to make. Even though he takes it out of the store, the salesman makes that just a *minor decision of trying it out.* If you change your mind—after all, you can bring it back! How do you think Sears got to be the biggest retail operation in the entire world? By being bashful about selling their products? No sir; I know from personal experience. I used to work for them!

So don't give your employee or your boss the chance to get off the hook once they've gone for the bait. Play him skillfully and you'll land him. Slip it on his account. Get him to agree on a minor point. Soon you'll find he'll be agreeing to your whole major proposition before he actually knows that he's flopping on the bank!

The six essentials of punching his button.

1. *The opening.* Get your listener's attention by fitting it in with his train of thought. This is important. Jump on his train; don't make him transfer to yours. Establish a point of contact with his interests—with what he wants. Excite his curiosity; get him to want to know more. *Get his attention.*

2. *The description or the explanation.* Tell him your idea or give him your order by first outlining its fundamental important features, then by filling in the necessary details so he'll fully understand what you want him to do. *Arouse his interest.*

3. *Give him the motive.* Create a desire in him to do it. Incite him to want—not just your proposition—but what it will do for him; the comfort, the pleasure, the profit he'll get from it. Make his mouth water. *Fan the flame of desire.*

4. *The proof or the guarantee.* Back up your idea or your order with proof positive so he can see how he'll benefit from your proposition. *Keep the fire burning!*

5. *The snapper or the penalty* will get immediate action for you. If he hesitates about making a decision, even on a minor point, show him—tactfully, of course—how he'll lose money or prestige or opportunity to get ahead *if he doesn't act now!*

6. *The close.* Now that your spadework is done, tell him just what to do and how to do it. Make it easy for him to act immediately. Use the assumptive closing sales technique. *Induce him to take action* by making it seem like the natural thing to do!

Everyone's a salesman.

You say you're a supervisor—not a salesman? You're an executive, a manager, and you don't sell anything? How'd you sell your wife on the idea of living with you the rest of her life? You told her about all the benefits she'd enjoy; didn't you? How'd you get your last raise? You sold your boss on what an outstanding job you were doing—on what a brilliant executive you were—right? Everybody's a salesman—including your own children!

A preacher is a salesman. He sells you on the idea of putting more money in the collection plate so he can build an addition on the church. He tells you about all the benefits you're going to get—even that invisible reward of heaven. He's selling you an intangible, and that takes a lot more salesmanship than you'll need. You're selling tangible benefits.

Remember Russell Conwell? He learned his lesson in his father's store. He went on to sell people so well from the pulpit on the idea of a college in Philadelphia that Temple University became a reality. He was its founder and first president.

Army officers are salesmen. They sell their programs to Congress to get bigger defense appropriations.

The President of the United States is a salesman. He spends most of his time trying to sell Congress his budget programs.

Your children are salesmen. They sell you every year—for about three weeks just before Christmas—about how good they've been for the past twelve months.

Dale Carnegie said, "There is only one way under high heaven to get anybody to do anything . . . and that is by making the other person want to do it. . . .":

Isn't that salesmanship? Persuasion? The art of getting through to people?

"If there's a single universal key to success, it lies in the ability to command the cooperation of people," says Irving I. Stone, president of the American Greetings Corporation, one of the country's largest greeting card firms.

You'll never command the cooperation of others unless you *sell them your ideas first.* Take it from me; if you want to go from supervisor to president of your corporation, *learn to sell your ideas*! Mr. Stone made it to the president's position, and he started lower than supervisor, too.

In short, everybody's a salesman, even a hermit. He had to sell himself on the idea of living alone.

To recapitulate . . . . .

Always sell your employee on your orders by showing him the benefits he'll gain by following them. Tell him what's in it for him. Beat him to the punch by telling him before he can ask you. You'll benefit by having employees who will–

1. *Do things right the first time.*
2. *Save time and money by avoiding costly mistakes.*
3. *Cooperate with you in every way.*

When you punch your boss's right button, you can get–

1. *A promotion,*
2. *A bonus,*
3. *A raise.*

To punch his button, use these six steps,

1. *The opening to get his attention.*
2. *The description or explanation to arouse his interest.*
3. *The motive to fan the flame of desire.*
4. *The proof or guarantee to keep the fire burning.*
5. *The snapper or the penalty to speed up his decision.*
6. *The close to induce him to take the action you want.*

Everybody's a salesman. Some are good—some are bad—some are better. May you be the best!

THE 12TH SECRET

Always Use the K-I-S-S Rule!

Shortly after I was commissioned a second lieutenant of infantry away back in World War II, I reported for duty to the 44th Division in Fort Lewis, Washington. There, because of the shortage of captains (which is something I never understood; when I was a lieutenant, there were never enough captains to go round. When I became eligible to be promoted to captain—there were too many, the General said, so I had to wait!) I was assigned to command Company E, 2nd Battalion, 71st Infantry.

I waited in the orderly room while First Lieutenant Schneider—who was headed for overseas—cleaned out the desk that was soon to be mine. Like all other army desk-users, he had his name-sign on it. But I noticed his was a bit out of the ordinary. On its backside—where he could see it plainly when he sat down—stenciled in huge black letters, was the word, *K-I-S-S!*

"What does that mean?" I asked. "Does it have a romantic significance?"

"Hell, no!" he said emphatically, fixing me with that cold stare first lieutenants always reserve for second lieutenants. "I was a sergeant for fifteen years before they made me an officer.

"That word reminds me not to do the stupid things I've seen some of my company commanders do during those years. I've heard a lot of ridiculous orders in my day. I don't want to repeat them. That's why the word, *K-I-S-S*.

"It means: *Keep it simple, stupid!* It's a good rule. The sooner you learn it, the better. Some men in this company have good educations. Others can barely sign the payroll. A couple of them never had two pair of shoes until they came in the army.

"You have to make your pitch to the man with the least education. Just because he doesn't have a diploma, or he's not an ROTC graduate like you, don't think he can't soldier—he can! You can't use big four and five syllable words with him, that's all. Tell him to *accomplish the mission* and he won't move. Tell him to *do the job* and he'll hop right to it.

"It boils down to this. Make your orders so simple he'll understand you. If he knows what you want, everyone else will, too. Do that—you'll have no problems. If you don't keep it simple—you won't last a month as company commander!"

I've used Lieutenant Schneider's *K-I-S-S rule* ever since—both in and out of the military. In fact, I used it so well in Company E, I almost had to stop using it so I could get a new assignment and get promoted!

I've benefited greatly throughout the years by using that simple rule. Now let me show you how *you can K-I-S-S, and benefit, too!*

Your subordinates work more effectively when they know exactly what their job is, and what you expect them to do.

Often a man's failure to do a decent job stems from his not being able to understand exactly what you want. Tell him precisely what you want and when you want it.

Your employees will respond to clear, concise orders that are simple and easy to understand. They'll be able to do things right the first time.

Don't overstate your order by including a mass of cumbersome details. Tell him what you want and when you want it, but let him figure out *how* to do it himself. When you do this, you'll develop a sense of responsibility in your subordinates by making each one a member of the team. No one'll be left sitting on the bench.

Apply the K-I-S-S rule to your own actions; you'll simplify your own work.

Most of us complicate our own jobs unnecessarily. Use the K-I-S-S rule, and you'll force yourself to get rid of trivia and red tape.

Now for a bird's eye view of how to do it. Here's what to loo . for in this chapter:

1. *Guidelines for simple orders.* (What you should do.)
2. *How to use SHOW AND TELL instead of formal orders.*
3. *Guidelines for following orders.* (What good employees want to do.)

GUIDELINES FOR SIMPLE ORDERS

1. The first guideline is the name of the game: K-I-S-S!

Don't complicate it.

No law says you have to use big words when you write or talk. If you think you have to use big words to prove you're the boss—forget it. Your people know you're the boss; you don't have to prove it.

You can use lots of small words to say what you mean. When you use small words, chances are everyone will know exactly what you mean. That's the purpose of communication—to let the other fellow know what you mean. Nothing else; at least, in this business.

The trouble with big words is they get in the way of what you really want to say. When you're through—no one knows for sure what you actually wanted him to do. Income tax instructions are always classics of confusion. I've seen army orders and corporation correspondence that would curl your hair and steam up your glasses, too.

Take this one, for instance. It's part of a regulation governing the absence of civil service employees for sickness at a Midwest air force base.

One sentence – 120 words!

Sick leave shall be granted to civil service employees at this air force base only when they are incapacitated for the normal performance of their duties by sickness, injury, or pregnancy and confinement, or for medical, dental, or optical examination or treatment, or when a dependent in the immediate family living with the employee is afflicted with a contagious disease which requires the care and attendance of said employee, or when, through previous exposure to such contagious disease, the presence of the employee at his regular place of duty would jeopardize the health and welfare of his fellow employees, or others who might be required to come into contact with said employee during the normal performance of their official duties.

"We're thinking about revising our directive governing sick leave for civilian personnel," the civil service director said. "Had too many complaints about it. For some reason people can't seem to understand it. Don't know why; perfectly clear to me!"

Well, he might just as well have said, "I've got my mind made up; don't confuse me with facts!"

2. Issue orders in a way that shows you expect immediate compliance.

A simple direct order lends itself to immediate obedience. A complicated one does not. Other factors enter the picture, too. Some say it's that quiet, but unmistakable, ring of authority—that indefinable something that's heard in your voice. Others feel it's a result of the faith a man has in his own abilities; the trust he puts in himself.

"In the quarter of a century I've been with General Electronics, I cannot recall a single case of disobedience of my orders," says Leslie Seamonds, superintendent of their Eastern Division. "But I never gave any man a reason to disobey. That's important! I never asked anyone to do anything that was embarrassing or degrading; nor did I ever ask a man to do something I wouldn't or couldn't do.

"The thought of a man disobeying my orders never entered my mind. It never occurred to me he might not obey me. I always acted as if he would do what I wanted him to immediately. He always did.

"I think he obeyed me for the same reason I obeyed my superiors: Respect; a mutual respect we felt for each other."

Which brings me to my next point, and that is—

3. Respect — or the lack of it — is the biggest reason a man will — or will not — obey you.

Treat a man with respect—he'll return your respect with obedience. If you do not respect him, he'll not obey you. It's just that simple. Look at this example.

In Europe, in 1919 after the end of World War I, sixty thousand men of the United States Army revolted against authority at St. Aignan-sur-Cher, France.

The conditions that had been allowed to develop by indifferent commanders were deplorable. Many men had been battle casualties. Some had been discharged from hospitals before their wounds were healed. The food was abominable. The camp was short of firewood and other supplies. Men were sleeping on the ground in freezing weather with only a pair of blankets apiece. The death toll from influenza, pneumonia, and the aggravation of battle wounds rose daily.

When General Pershing visited the camp, he relieved the commander on the spot and sent for a General Malone to take over the camp and restore order.

General Malone immediately set about relieving the physical hardship of the men. He recognized that the lack of discipline was an effect—not a cause. As he walked around the camp talking to the men, he said time after time, "I'm your new general. *I respect you, but I expect you to respect me!*"

He said nothing else and took no other action, but within less than 48 hours, sixty thousand rebellious men were again doing their duty, and doing it properly. *All because their new general showed them some courtesy and respect!*

4. Never issue an order you cannot enforce — a decision you cannot support — a promise you cannot keep.

Many people in authority fail here. They give their subordinates impossible jobs to do because they're afraid of failure themselves. They want to pass that failure on to someone else.

Give a man an order you cannot enforce, make a decision you cannot support, a promise you cannot keep, and you're not doing your job. *You're passing the buck.*

"I can't understand my boss," said Terry S., shift supervisor in the mill department of the M. Tire Company. "He just got through telling me he'd promised the cord wrapping department foreman five rolls of cover material by 7 p.m. and for me to deliver it on time.

"That's two thousand yards of material. I can process 300 yards an hour. It's 4 o'clock now. If nothing goes wrong, I still can't produce more than 900 yards in the next three hours. But I'll still be more than one thousand yards short. I can't keep his promise for him; I can't deliver the goods on time!"

The problem? Fear of criticism or failure caused a foreman to make a promise he couldn't keep. He passed the buck by issuing an order he could not enforce. But he'll blame the supervisor for not obeying his orders!

5. Follow up on every order.

Supervision is the key to this guideline. Supervisors supervise. So do executives, managers, admirals, and generals, but they give it a different name. *Inspect.* Sounds more impressive. Don't be fooled by semantics. The end result should be the same.

"Call the Commanding General. Tell him to meet the 5th Army Commander at Forney Air Field in 30 minutes. It is now 0630," crackled the radio in the control tower.

"Roger," answered the Fort Leonard Wood radio operator. He reached for the hot line that went straight to the CG's quarters.

"General Funston," he said. "The 5th Army Commander will be landing here at 0700. He wants you to meet him. It's now 0632, sir. Yes sir, I'll notify the staff duty officer."

At 0715, General Scott, the three-star 5th Army Commander, stood on the bumper of a 2-1/2 ton army cargo carrier in the post motor-pool, checking its oil level.

The rest of his staff, all competent and well qualified technicians, had scattered throughout the sprawling post on their unannounced surprise visit—the CMMI, Command Maintenance Materiel Inspection. Commanders at all levels were watching those inspectors with bated breath. Even General Funston, two-star general though he was, nervously watched his superior as he wiped the oil dipstick on a mechanic's rag, and rightly so. More army officers, even generals, have been relieved of command after a CMMI than all other reasons combined.

I was intrigued, not only at seeing a two-star general with the jitters, but also at the sight of a three-star general checking the oil level of an army truck, especially at 7:15 in the morning. It just seemed so out of place with what I thought generals were supposed to do in the army.

"Does a three-star general get paid for being a mechanic?" I whispered to his aide, Major Comstock.

"Hardly," the Major said, holding his answer to a whisper, too. "He only does this a couple of times a year. But those three stars make an impression that lasts for darn near a year. No one wants to get caught short the second time.

"He only spot-checks, anyway. Just a few trucks and tanks here and there. Only looks at stuff that's easy to check. Simple things like the oil, water, battery, things like that. He leaves the technical things to his staff.

"But he can get a darned good idea of the combat readiness of his command by looking under the hood himself, and that's what he's interested in. Combat readiness. If they're not combat ready, it means someone's not following orders."

So follow up; supervise—inspect. See that your employees are doing the job—doing what they're supposed to do—what you want them to do. You don't have to be a technician to supervise. You can learn a lot by checking fundamentals. Know the answers before you inspect. Don't get caught short yourself.

6. An order should have but one object; it should stay on course.

It's true you can issue orders with more than one objective, but when you do, it's no longer a simple order. Nor should it be oral; it should be written. Define each objective as an intermediate goal which must be reached before attainment of the final one.

This applies to written orders only. Oral orders must have only one object. Don't look for trouble. You get enough without asking for more.

7. Oral orders must be repeated back to you.

This is a rule. Never violate it. Don't bypass it. When you do—you'll fail. When your subordinate does not repeat your order, it will almost always result in misunderstanding and hard feelings.

Sometimes a man will balk about repeating your orders. He'll think you're insulting his intelligence. So be it! He'll just have to feel that way. He'll get over it.

I've given you few rules in this book. I believe in the use of skill—not rules, but this is one time I won't back down. *Oral orders must always be repeated back to you.* That's a rule!

8. Disguise your orders as suggestions or requests.

If your men have any initiative, you'll get better results from suggestions than from direct orders. Issue orders as a last resort. When you hand out orders right and left, you're acting like a line sergeant in a basic training camp. Don't do it.

Let him think it's his own idea.

"The best way to get a job done is to let the other fellow think it was his idea," says Bill Miller, a General Foods foreman. "For instance, one supervisor of mine is especially susceptible.

"If I want to get something done, I'll call him in on Monday and say, 'Glenn, I've been thinking about reversing number 3 machine. Might speed up production. Think it over a few days and give me your opinion. OK?'

"A couple of days later he'll burst into my office and say, 'Bill, I just had a brainstorm. Let's reverse the number 3 machine. It'll speed up our production!'

"Works every time. I get what I want; Glenn thinks every department improvement is his idea. What the heck, I don't mind giving him the credit. He does a better job for me when I do. That's all I want."

SHOW AND TELL

Use the SHOW AND TELL technique as a simple substitute for formal orders.

The audiovisual field has become so specialized in the past few years it's now a distinct field of study leading to a bachelor's degree. But the principle of *show and tell* is not new. It's as old as the prehistoric drawings found in caves in southwestern France and the Spanish peninsula. Some of these drawings are at least ten thousand, some probably twenty-five thousand years old. But they weren't getting college degrees for their work in those days.

We always think we're discovering something new. Usually it's *rediscovery*. For instance, an English firm, the Inca Construction Company, has come up with a *new* building system of interlocking cinderblock-size plastic bricks. You don't need brick laying skills to use them. They clip together, top to bottom, to form a watertight, load-bearing wall.

How new is that idea? Where did they get it? You can guess from their name—*Inca*. The Incas of Peru used that construction technique centuries ago when they clipped giant granite blocks together to build their houses and temples, many of which still stand.

An old proverb says, in effect, "The more a thing changes—the more it remains the same!" Even teen-agers!

The military uses show and tell.

The army saves millions of your tax dollars by using mockups of weapons in training, movies and slides to teach and demonstrate tactics and other military subjects. They can conduct highly specialized training using a closed circuit TV system. One technician in a centralized location can teach any number of students saving hundreds of thousands of dollars in costly equipment and instructors' salaries.

In one army base I visited, the closed circuit TV system is used to give five thousand trainees simultaneous instruction in five army theaters. The men never see their instructor. He's the technician who runs the central TV transmission point. Company cadre with the unit answer any questions. The only limitations on this kind of instruction are the number of TV monitors and the size of classrooms.

A scaled down style is used in elementary schools in their *Show and Tell Periods*. Of course, with small fry, they're learning how to present the subject as well as absorb it. This is good. I have a youngster who is more at home in front of an audience at twelve years of age than I was at twenty!

The show and tell method is easily adapted to business or industrial use. It's especially valuable when you're teaching new employees the use of highly complicated machinery or sophisticated electronic gear.

Zenith Corporation uses a show and tell method in a sixteen-week training course they conduct for all new employees who'll be working on their assembly lines.

There are eighteen general steps in the system. They can be tailored to fit your own operation, no matter whether you're conducting highly specialized training like Zenith, or individual instruction right at the machine. They're general enough to fit any operation—yet specific enough to help put together a Heathkit or a Dynaco amplifier.

The Eighteen Steps of Show and Tell.

1. Give detailed instructions to your employees, either oral or written.
2. Be sure that your "students" know the *why* and *how* of the operation.
3. Inform them of the standards you'll expect them to meet.

4. Give them sufficient time to attain those atandards.
5. Give instruction primary emphasis; production—secondary emphasis at first.
6. Supervise and inspect closely and constantly.
7. See that each employee is performing the task correctly.
8. Learn each step completely before going on to the next.
9. Reteach and redemonstrate wher necessary.
10. Stress speed and accuracy after the procedure is learned.
11. Make the instruction realistic at all times.
12. Ask pertinent questions to determine individual progress.
13. Be patient. Encourage a new employee by praise.
14. See that he observes all safety precautions.
15. Show a definite and positive interest in his progress.
16. Have the fast learners help the slow learners.
17. Help a man to evaluate his own performance.
18. Rotate a man from one job to another if appropriate.

GUIDELINES FOR FOLLOWING ORDERS

Most books I've read on motivation, supervision, executive development, and leadership have a chapter or so devoted to the issuance of orders by the man in command, the leader himself. They tell him how to do it and what to expect from the man below. They're written from the leadership viewpoint; i.e., *looking down from above.*

I've never seen a book written only on *followership;* I don't think I ever will. Followership is not a popular subject. No one wants to train to be a follower; everyone wants to be the leader.

I don't intend to write a book on followership, either. But I am going to give you a few paragraphs here from the viewpoint of *looking up from below*—as if you were the boss and I were your employee *way down there.* Here's what I'll try to do for you.

1. I want to make sure I understand what you want.

I'll repeat your oral order back to you if you'll *take time to listen!* I want to do a good job for you because you're my boss and you're paying me. But I can't if your orders are ambiguous, vague, and incomplete. Then I have to guess at what you want, and I usually guess wrong. That's why you think I'm disobedient sometimes.

Sure, I make mistakes. But they're honest mistakes. If I were viciously and maliciously violating your orders, you'd have a right to fire me, but I'm not. I'm trying my level best to help you. But I can't unless you *tell me exactly what you want me to do. That's not too much to ask, is it?*

2. Give me a job within my capabilities to do for you.

Please don't ask me to do something I can't do and then get mad when I fail. When you know I can only produce 120 units an hour—why do you give me an order to produce 150 an hour? You know I can't do that—so why ask me to?

Please don't ask me to speed up my machine beyond its safety limits to meet your production goals and then chew me out when it breaks down or the quality falls below par.

3. When I ask for help — then help me!

If I see I won't be able to do the job you've given me to do, I'm going to call on you for help. If I don't, I'll only mire down and get nowhere.

4. I'll solve the problems for you as they come up.

I know sometimes things don't work out the way you had them planned. Sometimes, adjustments have to be made. And I'll do that. I'll make corrections—I'll add and subtract as necessary—*if you give me the authority to do so.*

But if you don't—you'll never be able to go home; you'll have to live in the plant or we can only run eight hours a day. We'll have to stop running three shifts around the clock. If you don't trust me—why don't you get rid of me?

You have to learn to depend on other people, boss. You know, if it hadn't been for men like Chief Boatswain's Mate L. M. Jahnsen who had the courage to do what he felt was right, we might never have recovered from the disaster of Pearl Harbor, boss. Or we wouldn't have this big plant you and I work in. You have a lot of good men just like Jahnsen working for you. All you have to do is look around; you'll find them. But let me tell you about him first.

He was only a garbage collector.

On the morning of Pearl Harbor, Chief Boatswain's Mate L. M. Jahnsen was skippering a garbage scow collecting refuse from the fleet when the Japanese attack started. As the hard hit West Virginia began to burn, Jahnsen headed his scow into the heat, the smoke, and the exploding ammunition from the battleship to direct a single fire hose into the flaming wreckage. He did what little he could to lessen the ruin of the Pacific Fleet.

"Oh, that was his duty," you say. No, it wasn't, boss. His duty was the unglamorous job of collecting garbage from the fleet. He could have pulled away from the danger area and watched in safety from the distance as a spectator. Many a man of lesser strength did just that. I know, boss; I was there. I was on the business end of that hose!"

In summary, then . . . .

To summarize, rather than repeating all the guidelines for you again, I'd like to say this.

It's the simple things that always last longest and wear best over the years. The simplest writing is always the best because it is easiest to understand. You don't need a dictionary to read and understand Hemingway's *Old Man and the Sea* as you might with some textbooks. Yet it received the Nobel Prize for Literature in 1954.

Nearly two thousand years ago a man who walked by the Sea of Galilee understood well this principle of simplicity. His teachings are still studied today. His name, of course, was Jesus Christ, and He is easily the most important figure who has ever appeared on the face of this earth. It makes no difference whether you consider Him to be the Son of God or just a sincere philosopher and teacher. However you look at Him, you must immediately admit that He has influenced the course of history more than any other man who has ever lived.

And everything in His life was simple: His clothing and His food; His language and His words. The message He left is thought by some to be highly complicated, or it has been complicated by them—which, I will not say. I am not a theologian, but I have my own opinion.

But I do know this. The orders He gave were simple, concise, and to the point when He said,

"Follow me."

From Now On You're the Big Boss

You might be the big boss already, for all I know, but if you're not, let's pretend that you are right now. For problem purposes in this exercise, and to make sure the school solution works, let's make you a branch plant manager in a corporation set-up.

Let's also suppose you're earning thirty thousand a year in that job. Now the corporation president up there in Chicago or Detroit or New York is going to be looking more closely at what you're doing than if you were earning only five thousand a year.

At five thousand a year, you're worth $2.50 an hour to the corporation. Chances are, at that level, you'd be doing a specific skilled or semi-skilled job. You might work with your hands or your feet or both, but your superiors wouldn't expect you to do much more than just a routine, ordinary day's work.

But when the corporation is paying you 15 dollars an hour—a total of 120 dollars a day to manage one of their plants—they're going to expect a lot more out of you. What will they be looking for specifically in you?

Your ability to handle people.

That's what they'll be looking for. Any skilled workman, say, a bricklayer, for example, is limited as to how much he can earn in a year as long as he remains a bricklayer. If he decides to become a contractor, that's a different story. But you're not a bricklayer, and the corporation president doesn't expect you to act like one.

He expects you to surround yourself with a competent staff, first of all. And he expects you to delegate the proper tasks to the proper people, to see to it that their work is properly supervised, and still have time left over to devote to those aspects of your job which you, and you alone, can do.

So your ability to handle people becomes extremely important, especially when that corporation president is hundreds of miles away—not across the hall or down the corridor. How important is that ability? Well, let's see what a couple of other successful businessmen have to say about managing people.

Don Thompson, manufacturing executive for General Electric, worded that idea this way: "No matter how much work a man can do individually, he will not advance if he doesn't know how to control others."

Harry Wriggs, executive vice-president of Channelmaster Corporation, an electronics firm that could've made your TV antenna, says this: "Even if you can't drive a nail—even if you have no mechanical ability whatever—your future will be assured if you know how to manage people."

In business, in the military, anywhere—that means knowing how to—

Delegate responsibility to your subordinate.

Before you can do that, you must make sure you've developed a sense of responsibility in that subordinate. Here's what you'll gain when you know how to do that:

You'll develop a competent staff when you show them you have faith in them—when you indicate that you expect them to do their best for you.

People tend to perform according to what's expected of them, they'll try to reach your standards. If they know you have confidence in them to do a first-rate job, that's what they'll always try to give you.

You'll gain the trust and respect of your subordinates when you delegate responsibility for the details of the job to them.

You're not doing a real job as a boss unless you delegate responsibility for the details to your subordinates. If you insist on keeping your hand in everything, you'll discourage your men by literally competing with them.

Not only that, by doing everything yourself, you keep your subordinates from learning how to make their own decisions. Sooner or later, the best ones will quit; the rest will sit back and let you do all the work while they watch. (If you're still around—that is!)

You'll encourage each subordinate to use initiative and to cooperate wholeheartedly when you give him a chance to take part in decisions.

When your people feel they've had a say in a decision, they'll cooperate with you by supporting that decision. They'll look at it as their own, so they'll back it to the hilt.

Even if they don't agree fully, they'll still back your decision more strongly simply because you gave them a chance to give their own viewpoints. Of course, you should always give full and fair consideration to their ideas and allow them to express their opinions freely.

Develop a sense of responsibility in your subordinate and you'll encourage a mutual confidence, trust, and respect between the two of you.

Motivate a man by showing him you trust him, and he'll respond with everything he's got for you. When you build a man's confidence in himself and in his abilities to do a job for you, you'll automatically increase his feeling of responsibility toward you and the company.

Benjamin Fairless, former chairman of U. S. Steel, said, "I pick out people whom I can trust to do things right and to whom I can delegate authority."

In this chapter I'll show you how to develop a sense of responsibility in your subordinates so you can delegate that authority to them. Keep in mind, please, you're the manager of a corporation's branch plant in this chapter. You're the big boss!

So you should be thinking in terms of training your immediate staff—developing top assistants who are going to help you run the whole show. You're not a shift supervisor or a department foreman now. You're not the chief of the industrial engineering section or even a production superintendent. You're the manager, the chief, the boss, the wheel. Now you've got nowhere else to pass the buck. *The buck ends with you.*

If you want to develop a group of staff members who will do their best, you'll have to work closely with each one of them. I want to give you several guidelines to follow that will help you develop just such a group of qualified staff assistants. Remember, they can make you or break you, so it's important that you pick the right ones.

1. How to choose your staff assistants.

Often, a man's previous specialty will be a contributing factor in his selection. However, in many plants, the organizational set-up almost precludes the controller, say for example, from ever becoming the plant manager. It shouldn't be that way.

Judge a man by his ability to control people.

The best department foreman shouldn't be your only choice for your new production superintendent or your assistant manager just because he knows more about the physical production than anyone else in the plant. If you arbitrarily box a man in because of his previous specialty alone, you can overlook some top notch managerial talent. So judge a man by his ability to manage people, not books, arithmetic, or production lines; or battalions or regiments either.

General Lucius Clay summed up that idea quite aptly when he joined Continental Can Company. The general, well known for his exceptionally able administrative ability in the military, was being interviewed by a reporter about his new civilian position.

"Do you know anything about civilian industry?" the reporter asked.

"No, I do not," the general replied.

"Then what makes you think you'll succeed in business?" asked the reporter. "You don't know anything at all about manufacturing cans, do you?"

"No, I don't," said the general. "And I don't know how to lay an egg, either, but I sure know how to smell a rotten one!"

So choose a man for his managerial abilities—for his talent in handling people. That's why Continental Can chose General Clay. You don't have to base your decision on the past alone. If he's to be promoted from within, you can test his potential management abilities by some specific assignments before you make your final decision. General George C. Marshall chose Dwight Eisenhower for future top command assignments as a general when Eisenhower was still a major!

You and your staff must mesh.

"When I first took command of the 2nd Battalion, 2nd Training Regiment at Fort Leonard Wood, my executive officer asked if I wanted to be the good guy or the bad guy," says Colonel Martin L. Pitts.

"Since I'd been an exec before myself, I knew exactly what he was driving at. One of us had to be the hatchet man. It was just a matter of deciding which one of us it would be. We couldn't both play the part of the hero. One of us had to be the villain!"

Even though you want your staff and your top assistants to represent you, let them fill complementary roles. They don't have to be mirror images or your identical twin to do the job for you.

Two dynamic and aggressive people, especially in managerial positions of heavy responsibility, could be at it hammer and tongs in a week or so. That's why most lasting marriages are those where interests interlace and mesh, but are not necessarily identical. In fact, it's better if they're not.

If your interests are too much alike, you'll be doing the same things together 24 hours a day, and even the best of companions can become monotonous. It's nice to be able to play a round of golf or bowl just with the boys once in a while. Togetherness can be a wonderful thing, but I also appreciate a little privacy and a chance to express my individuality. I'm sure you do, too.

So you'll find that your most capable assistants will be those whose strengths match your weaknesses and vice versa. The end result should give you an impregnable wall of strength.

2. Qualities to look for in your staff.

"I want a man who's 25 years old with his military service behind him, married so that that he's settled down and dependable and has obligations to meet, a college graduate, preferably with a master's degree—and with at least *20 years of experience!*" says Arthur Harper, chief of Westinghouse's personnel division.

"All joking aside though, we do want a specific kind of individual for our management positions. He should be the kind who wants to learn and who can be quick about it. It's a fast track for executives today. He should be able to think for himself and he needs to have some good judgement and common sense.

"Since he'll be in a top level managerial position eventually, he'll need the ability to work with people at all levels, to get along with them, to gain their confidence. But he doesn't have to know how to do all this when he comes to us. We'll teach him how to manage.

"If he's anxious to succeed and if he has a sincere desire to learn we can teach him the skills of management, such as planning and organizing his work and supervising the work of others. We'll show him how to handle that additional responsibility and authority that he wants."

Make him responsible for training new employees.

One of the best ways to teach a new man management skills is to give him the responsibility of supervising the training program for your new employees. Being responsible for teaching others will force him to learn every aspect of the various departments in the plant. Even if the practical work aspects of your training program are conducted on the job, giving him the overall responsibility for supervising that program will give him an understanding of your whole operation that would be hard for him to gain in any other way.

3. Always give him all the straight facts.

Don't play hard to get or try to be coy with your assistant manager or your immediate staff. This is an important principle to follow in developing a sense of responsibility in them. Don't hold anything back. Give him a clear and concise picture of exactly what he's expected to do and what you actually expect from him.

He must know what details he can handle without conferring with you and which matters you insist on keeping the final say-so for yourself. Let him know exactly where his authority begins and ends.

One of the best ways to do this is to have a job description written for his position. If there is none, give him some general guidance and let him write it. It's a good exercise to help a man determine the limits of his responsibility and authority himself. Of course, you'll be expected to correct and grade his paper.

I never cease to be amazed at the high salaried management positions that do not have even a broad delineation of a man's duties and responsibilities. Such a job description should not limit a man's initiative, but he is entitled to know what his minimum responsibilities are.

If I have the responsibility for doing a certain task, I want to know about it. Tell me before the milk is spilled, not afterward! If I do not have the responsibility for a certain task, then I want to know that, too. A definition of boundaries must be made for your assistants. No two baseball parks are alike in the major leagues. There are different ground rules for each one, but both teams are informed as to what they are before the game starts—not after it's in progress.

4. Smooth his path with an SOP (Standing Operating Procedure).

I've already mentioned that one of the biggest headaches an assistant manager or a staff member has is knowing which matters should be given to the boss for a final decision and which ones he may handle himself.

An SOP will take care of most of these questions for you. An SOP could vary in size from one or two pages to a thick volume with hundreds of pages. Just remember this: The thicker the SOP—the greater will be your reader's resistance!

You can use an SOP to prevent problems.

"A good SOP will solve most of your problems on the production line. It'll cover the operation and maintenance of most of your machinery. It encompasses most of the detailed operation and that's as it should be," says Walter Park, manager of a Chrysler assembly plant in St. Louis.

"Oh, it won't answer all your subordinate's questions nor will it solve all his problems. His biggest question is always to be—*Should the boss know about this?* A good SOP will answer that question for him. If you're the boss, and if all the correspondence and paperwork falls on your back, as it does on mine, then *your immediate staff is entitled to know what papers you must see and what correspondence you have to sign.* If your assistant manager knows that, he'll also know automatically *what you don't have to see and what you don't have to sign!*

"To give guidance to my people in these two touchy areas, I put out this little memo which I call, 'Keep the Boss Informed.' Each department or section head has a copy of it on his desk. Each supervisor carries a copy in his pocket."

KEEP THE BOSS INFORMED.

I want the following matters brought to my personal attention at once.

1. Any *important* subject that will require some *immediate action* on my part which is not specifically covered in some previously published policy or directive.

2. Letters of disapproval of any sort from my superiors.

3. Any and all errors, irregularities, or deficiencies in this plant's operation that have been pointed out by my superiors.

4. Any letters or reports that indicate neglect or dereliction of duty on the part of anyone in this plant, or that carry even the slightest hint of criticism, censure, or reprimand.

5. Written appeals made by any subordinate about decisions that I or my staff or anyone else in management has made.

6. Any subject that would injure the good name or reputation of the corporation or our plant.

7. Any *serious* accidents or incidents, on or off duty, which involve plant personnel.

8. Any reports of financial irregularities or discrepancies or any shortage of property or materials.

The following matters will be sent to me for my personal action and/or my personal signature.

1. Any non-routine letter or report that contains a request or a recommendation to be made to my superiors.

2. Letters or certificates of commendation, award, or appreciation that are to be given to any employee.

3. Any letter or report that will cast a shadow of doubt on the good name or reputation of any person or any department in the plant.

4. Letters of disapproval or negative replies on requests or suggestions from subordinates.

5. Any letter that contains the slightest hint of criticism, censure, or reprimand.

6. Letters or reports to be sent to any governmental agency.

7. Letters and reports that have to do with future planning.

8. Any letters and reports of *exceptional or outstanding information* not specifically covered in this memorandum.

"This isn't a cure-all," Walter says, "but when people know exactly what matters I want to know about, and specifically which papers to route through my office, it answers 95 percent of their questions. It speeds up their work and my desk is kept comparatively clear, too."

I've seen a lot of SOP's in my time, both bad and good—short and long—simple and complicated. I've never seen a better one (or a shorter one) than Walter's. As he says, it won't solve all the problems, but if it would—you and I both might be out of a job, and so would Walter Park, too.

5. Keep your staff informed.

If your assistant is to do a good job for you, you'll have to let him know what's going on. You have to run a mutual information program. Keep him informed of your plans, their progress, and your reasons for making each move. Let him know about your problems, too. See that he learns the ins and outs of working with people at all levels in your outfit, especially department heads and production foremen.

"If you pick a man to be your assistant and pay him for it, then you're a fool if you don't help develop his latent managerial abilities," says Harris Foster, a manager of one of General Dynamics' plants.

"Use him properly and you'll gain several hours weekly for your other managerial duties. A good assistant can take part of your work load off your shoulders. And you can develop a man who'll be able to step into your shoes if you get sick or the trout are biting in the high Rockies. Or just one afternoon a week for a round of golf would help break the tension for you."

If you don't learn to use your staff, you'll never be able to have a single moment of peace. I don't think the manager lives who doesn't carry the plant home on his shoulders every night, but at least you can split the load. Two can worry a lot better than one!

6. Give him some working room.

Some managers make the mistake of trying to keep their fingers on every move that's made by their assistant staff members. This constant checking will make your people nervous; it will inhibit their development. Rather than cause an assistant to lose confidence in himself and his own abilities, it's far better to accept the fact that he's going to make some mistakes once in a while. He has no other way to learn. It's far better to hold a loose rein on him.

7. Teach him the theory of completed staff work.

An experienced staff assistant thinks his way carefully through each problem that you hand him to solve. He then decides upon a definite line of procedure to follow. He must decide what information he needs and which other staff members or department heads he needs to get in touch with to gather it. He has to consider every possible angle and the viewpoints of all interested parties before he reaches a final decision.

That's how an experienced staff assistant works. A young and inexperienced one won't be able to do it quite as easily and not nearly as quickly. The army in 1941 found itself in the position of having a great many enthusiastic and sincere, but horribly green and inexperienced, young staff officers.

To help the officers in the Corps of Military Police, the Provost Marshal General issued an order in January 1942 which stated in a thorough manner the theory of completed staff work. His memorandum soon found its way into every staff office in the army for its advice was invaluable. It has since been found in the navy and the air force and hundreds of civilian business offices. Since I was an infantry officer in World War II, I must admit that it's hard for me to praise anything the military police did, but I guess there has to be a first time for everything!

I'm indebted to General J. B. Sweet and to the Stackpole Company, Harrisburg, Pennsylvania for allowing me to quote this document. It has been taken from the 15th Edition of the Officer's Guide, February, 1950.

DOCTRINE OF COMPLETED STAFF WORK

"1. The doctrine of 'completed staff work' is a doctrine of this office.

2. 'Completed Staff Work' is the study of a problem, and presentation of a solution, by a staff officer, in such form that all that remains to be done on the part of the head of the staff division, or the commander, is to indicate his approval or disapproval of the completed action. The words 'completed action' are emphasized because the more difficult the problem is, the more the tendency is to present the problem to the chief in piecemeal fashion. It is your duty as a staff officer to work out the details. You should not consult your chief in the determination of those details, no matter how perplexing they may be. You may and should consult other staff officers. The product, whether it involves the pronouncement of a new policy or affects an established one, should, when presented to the chief for approval or disapproval, be worked out in finished form.

3. The impulse which often comes to the inexperienced staff officer to ask the chief what to do, recurs more often when the problem is difficult. It is accompanied by a feeling of mental frustration. It is so easy to ask the chief what to do, and it appears so

easy for him to answer. Resist that impulse. You will succumb to it only if you do not know your job. It is your job to advise your chief what he ought to do, not to ask him what you ought to do. He needs answers, not questions. Your job is to study, write, restudy and rewrite until you have evolved a single proposed action—the best one of all you have considered. Your chief merely approves or disapproves.

4. Do not worry your chief with long explanations and memoranda. Writing a memorandum to your chief does not constitute completed staff work, but writing a memorandum for your chief to send to someone else does. Your views should be placed before him in finished form so that he can make them his views simply by signing his name. In most instances, completed staff work results in a single document prepared for the signature of the chief, without accompanying comment. If the proper result is reached, the chief will usually recognize it at once. If he wants comment or explanation, he will ask for it.

5. The theory of completed staff work does not preclude a 'rough draft' but the rough draft must not be a half-baked idea. It must be complete in every respect except that it lacks the requisite number of copies and need not be neat. But a rough draft must not be used as an excuse for shifting to the chief the burden of formulating the action.

6. The 'completed staff work' theory may result in more work for the staff officer, but it results in more freedom for the chief. This is as it should be. Further, it accomplishes two things:

a. The chief is protected from half-baked ideas, voluminous memoranda, and immature oral presentments.

b. The staff officer who has a real idea to sell is enabled more readily to find a market.

7. When you have finished your 'completed staff work' the final test is this:

If you were the chief, would you be willing to sign the paper you have prepared, and stake your professional reputation on its being right?

If the answer is in the negative, take it back and work it over, because it is not yet 'completed staff work.' "

I have changed nothing from the original text in this quote. If you want to change some of the wording, please do so. Actually, about the only word you'll need to change is *officer*. You can substitute any civilian term you desire. This is the finest document I've ever seen to help a new staff man. And lots of old-timers could use it, too.

8. Grant him the necessary authority.

This is your last guideline, and if you've reached this stage of the game, you shouldn't really need it. If your staff is in the groove, and if they've got the pattern you want working, then let 'em loose once in a while. Turn 'em free and let 'em run! When you do, you'll find that the times you need to control and manage their actions will become the exception rather than the rule.

A few final words.

To summarize, I'd like to say that if you want to be the really big boss, you must have a basic ability to control and manage people. You must know how to delegate responsibility and authority, and then how to supervise to make sure it gets done. Develop your ability to lead others. It's your greatest asset and will lead you to success.

How to be Liked by Your Employees —
and Still be the Boss!

I've saved the two hardest chapters (for both of us, I think) to write until last, and it's almost a flip of the coin whether this chapter should come before or after the next one—*You Can't Win 'em All!*

However, I finally decided you ought to try out all the bait you could before you find out that once in a while you won't be able to hook one; or worse yet, he'll break your new line and get away from you. But now—to the subject at hand: *How to be liked by your employees—and still be the boss!*

Getting along with your employees and being liked by them while being the boss could be compared with wanting to have your cake and eating it, too. Almost, but not quite, impossible. It can be done when you know how.

Even the most autocratic of executives wants to be liked—at least a little, and at least by a few of his employees. Dale Carnegie discovered that, next to health, the main interest of grownups was developing their skills in their relationships with other people. They wanted to know the secret of how to get along with and how to influence other people.

Being liked by your employees normally means being respected by them, too. In fact, I don't think it's possible to like a person unless you do respect him. Even the high and the mighty, the rich and the powerful, still want to be liked and respected by their associates and their employees.

For example, I could tell you about an extremely rich real estate man, a Mr. Bob T., who is deeply bitter toward life in spite of all his money. "People don't like me; they don't respect me!" he complains.

"The hardest part of being a general and commanding a division is the loneliness," says Major General Edward Shumacher. True, but that's the way it has to be; it's never crowded on the mountain top. No matter how high a man goes, how rich he becomes, or how important he gets, he still longs for the sincere companionship of a few close friends he can trust. He still wants to be liked and respected.

So let's face it. Being the big boss is a tough proposition. Those who try to maintain control of their employees and be popular at the same time invariably lose. As I once heard a division production superintendent at Boeing Aircraft say, "Sure, I want to be liked and respected by my employees, but I'm not running in any popularity contest. I'm running a division for Boeing and that comes first."

139

You can't use popularity to win the long haul.

Popularity of songs and singers, Broadway actors and Hollywood movie stars comes and goes. It never remains constant. If you want to last, you have to be liked and respected for the long haul rather than go for some short-term popularity.

A girl who goes all the way in the back seat of your car might be popular with all the fellows for a while, but she's not the one you'll pick when you start looking around for a wife.

A postmaster might be temporarily popular with his letter carriers if he cancelled all mail deliveries on rainy days just to please them. But he wouldn't be doing his duty, and his employees would neither like nor respect him for doing it.

A frontline division commander who does not send out reconnaissance patrols to determine the enemy's strength and intentions might be momentarily popular, especially with those who didn't have to go, but he'll lose that popularity fast when a surprise attack slaughters one of his regiments.

Let me, therefore, point out that you owe a responsibility to your employees to require them to do those things which are for their own benefit—and for the benefit of you and your company, too; even though those requirements are not always popular. *The popular decision is not always the proper decision.*

And so—an end to popularity. I know I've discussed it at quite some length, but I did want you to be able to distinguish between it and being truly liked and respected by your employees. In case there's any final question in your mind, ask yourself these two questions. Would you be popular with your children if you let them stay home from school? How long would you be popular? So let's dispense with popularity completely; I'll not mention it again.

Will you gain any specific benefits by being liked by your employees even though you're the boss? Of course you will. Let me name off just a few of the benefits for you.

First of all, it's a good feeling just to have people like you—to feel that you're really wanted.

You won't have to put on a false front. You can simply be yourself.

You won't have to use soft soap and flattery and butter up your employees. Nor will you need to throw your weight around just to prove you're the boss.

You can just act normal. You won't have to indulge in any of those silly games so many people play in a vain attempt to impress others.

To get those benefits, all you have to do is follow these eight simple guidelines. You'll soon find out you can still be liked and respected by your employees in spite of being the boss.

1. Set the example to be followed.

If you want to set an example to be followed, and still be liked while you're doing it, let me give a few tips. First, don't make the mistake of putting yourself up on a pedestal. Don't be pompous and stuffy about it. That's no way to set the example. Don't try to save the world. Reformers and crusaders are often hard to swallow. A friend of mine, Howard S., an ex-drunk who got sober on the Alcoholics Anonymous program, told me this about how A.A. members set the example.

"A.A. works because nobody tries to shove it down your throat. *They don't tell you how to do it. They simply tell you how they did it.* In other words, it's all up to you. A.A. is like marriage. There it is if you want it—and there it is if you don't want it!"

So when you set the example for your employees to follow, don't try to remold the whole world to your pattern. Live and let live; easy does it. If you want to drink—that's your business; if John Jones wants to—that's his business as long as it doesn't interfere with his performance on the job.

If you want to smoke—that's your affair. If Harry Smith wants to—it's none of your business. In short, make yourself an example to be followed—but don't force people to follow you. Don't look at yourself as the model of excellence to be admired.

I could write a whole book on how to set the example. For instance, I could discuss the eleven cardinal principles of leadership. And I could tell you how you ought to develop the personal qualities of honesty, loyalty, courage, justice, and the like—but I won't. We have neither time nor space; so I'll just say this:

You must swim — but not get wet.

You must influence without being influenced. You must affect the actions of others without being affected yourself. You must stand as the symbol, the standard, the hallmark of excellence for your men to emulate. *You must drink—but not get drunk!*

"How can you set an example for your employees today?" a young junior executive with American Oil asked me. "If you don't smoke or drink or play around a little, they think you're a square—something out of the dark ages.

"You know, if you don't have a pad with a mistress stashed away somewhere—if you go home to your wife every night because you happen to love her and you believe in those old-fashioned marriage vows—*some people* think you belong in a zoo or a museum; maybe even an institution of some kind!"

Now that young man said only one thing I might possibly agree with. That's the phrase in italics—*some people!* But other than that, I can't agree. He's listening to the wrong voices. And sooner or later, if what they say bothers him, he'll be influenced by those voices.

What he doesn't realize is that those voices represent only the small minority. And no matter how much some of his employees and his associates might kid him about his *old-fashioned* (this time the italics are mine) Sunday School virtues, you can bet they wish they had the courage to practice them, too!

So stick to your principles; don't worry about what *you think your employee is thinking.* Chances are—he isn't! One last note of caution here before we leave this point. *Just set the example for yourself to follow; you're the only person whose morals you really have to worry about!*

2. Don't set up your own standards of right and wrong.

The previous guideline leads automatically into this one. But don't worry. I'm not going to turn this whole chapter into some high sounding moral treatise. I'm not a preacher, and anyway, there are plenty of good books which define moral codes into very explicit areas of good and evil—black and white—right and wrong. A couple of good examples can be found right in the Bible—the Ten Commandments and the Sermon on the Mount.

It's only when you and I decide to bend that code to fit our own private purposes that we run into trouble. And when we do try to bend it, we also try to get someone else to go along for the ride so we can justify our own actions.

For example, it wouldn't be at all fair of us to say that the Japanese were wrong in World War II unless we know that *right is a very definite and fixed principle or law* which they knew, too, and should have followed, but didn't.

But if they did not know the difference between right and wrong, then we could no more blame them for starting a war than we could blame them for the peculiar slant of their eyes. And the same would be said for the Nazis. (Except the eyes, of course.)

The thing is—they did know, and still they set up their own standards of right and wrong. You may not have to go to war in your own plant and fight a pitched battle with your employees, but I will guarantee you this. If you try to set up your own standards of right and wrong—if you try to live by some double standard of some sort, you'll have employees who won't like you or respect you. And you'll have a hard job holding down your position as the big boss, too.

3. Don't expect them to agree with everything you say or do.

Just as no two people have fingerprints exactly alike, neither do any of us have exactly the same ideas about religion, politics, or the opposite sex. We seldom can agree about anything, even the correct time of day. So respect the other man's opinion. Why try to prove that he's wrong—especially if he's one of your own employees? Don't start an argument; you never really gain a thing—now do you?

"You can't win an argument," says Curt Simonds, a division sales manager with Ampex. "I don't care whether it's one of your employees or a customer. If you win an argument with a customer—you lose! Why? Well, you lose a customer, that's why. And if you lose an argument with him, you still lose for when he proves his point and wins the argument—he'll have to take his business somewhere else. Otherwise he'd lose face with you. Either way, you lose the argument for you lose a customer. And customers are valuable to us. They keep us in business; we don't like to lose them.

"For example, sometimes we'll have a customer of long standing who suddenly decides he's going to stop buying from us. He might show our salesman some flashy competitive product and praise its good points. Naturally, he expects us to defend our own product, and we will. *But not by arguing with him!*

"I would praise the good features of the competition. Then I'd simply go on to tell him about the good points our own models have *over and above that competitive product.* But I'll never try to beat my competitor down by arguing about his product with my customer."

And you shouldn't start an argument either. You can't expect every man to agree with everything you do or say, even if he's your employee. He won't. He has a right to his own opinion, too. So don't argue with him. Even if he's a valued customer, you don't have to kowtow and agree with him just to keep him as a customer, but you should always respect his opinion. You'll be able to keep him as a friend ninety-nine times out of a hundred, and probably a customer, too, when you do.

In the end, there's only one way to win an argument; avoid it. And you're a long way from getting into one if you'll just remember that you are not the final authority on very much of anything. Only one individual on this earth was perfect, and they crucified Him. If you're not perfect—yet you still persist in saying that you're right every time—what do you think they'll do to you?

4. Make allowances for inexperience.

A twenty-game winner in professional baseball doesn't get that way overnight. He spends hundreds of hours throwing at a target first. And so does a winning quarterback. Every top professional started his career as an amateur. He has to gain experience somewhere.

So don't criticize a man when he's new and honestly trying. Would you criticize the bride or the groom if they make a mistake during their wedding ceremony, especially if it's their first marriage? The man who never tries never makes any mistakes, but he never gets anything done, either.

"I hate to see a good piece of material ruined because of a new operator's inexperience," says Lewis Gates, a supervisor with the Farrah Manufacturing Company, "but my getting mad about it doesn't help the situation one bit. It won't save the cloth, and it just makes the person even more nervous and more prone to make another mistake.

"So I usually try to smooth it over by telling the person not to worry about it, and just to keep trying. I guess that's why they still make pencils with erasers, isn't it?"

5. Always be considerate.

Treat every male employee like a gentleman and every woman like a lady. Few things will contribute more to building a hard working and efficient team than a boss who's considerate about the feelings of his people.

Be calm and courteous toward every subordinate. Consider the effects on them of any decisions you might make. Take into account their problems, both on and off the job—business and personal. Do everything you can to build up a person's self-respect.

"I'd been trying for close to a year to sell an insurance policy to a wealthy doctor in Cumberland, Wisconsin," sales Michael Scott. "Although the doctor and I'd gotten to be real friendly, I'd never been able to put a dent in him when it came to insurance. One day he suggested that he and his wife and I have dinner together that night. 'Maybe you can sell her,' he laughed, 'but I doubt it. She's got even more sales resistance than I have!'

"The next day he called me. 'Drop by my office,' he said, 'and bring along a policy application. You sold my wife last night.'

"How?" I asked. "We didn't even discuss insurance!"

" 'By your simple old-fashioned courtesy,' he said. 'You simply called her *Ma'am* each time you spoke to her. It struck a nostalgic chord in her and she loved you for it!' "

A simple matter of old-fashioned courtesy and respect. Oh, I wouldn't recommend calling a young lady who's in her teens or her twenties—even her thirties—*Ma'am,* but you'd be surprised how flattered an older lady will be when you use that title. And the younger the man, the more pleased she'll be.

If you do happen to have any ardent, young, unmarried females in your company who've got their eyes on you, you'll be pleasantly surprised at how fast the word, *Ma'am,* when used with deference and respect, can put out those flames of desire and conquest!

Always be consistent.

To be considerate of your employees, always be consistent. If you fly off the handle at any little thing, you'll frighten them into their shells, and they'll be afraid to make a move. No one cares to invite the boss's bad temper down on their heads. People follow well only the leader whose course is steady and whose actions are dependable and predictable.

No one likes to work where there is disorder and chaos; no man appreciates mob rule. Everyone likes to work where things are done properly, orderly, and efficiently with as little confusion and distraction as possible. That's why people will discipline themselves and accept your punishment when they make a mistake just as long as that punishment is both considerate and consistent.

No price is too high if the price is first known.

6. Give ground on trifles — never on principles.

Be flexible. Be willing to give ground occasionally on a minor matter. The strong oak tree refuses to accept the buffeting of the typhoon as it roars across the islands of the

Pacific so it is torn from its roots to die. The bamboo, slight of stature and not nearly as strong as the oak, bends with the wind and survives the wild carnage of nature.

Too many supervisors refuse to yield on unimportant details, saying there's a principle involved. *The trouble is—nine times out of ten, that principle is pride!* This always reminds me of the fellow who keeps on trying to collect on a bad poker debt. "It's not the money that's important," he says. "It's the principle of the thing!" My eye—it's the money that's the principle to him!

7. You must see — and be seen!

If you want your people to like you and respect you, they must know who you are. You must go and see for yourself what is being done, how it's being done, and who's doing it.

A comfortable seat behind a desk is a poor place to stay if you want your people to know who you are. Don't look at your desk as your place of business. It's only one small tool to help you conduct your business. You don't even need a room to call an office. Your real office should be in your head.

Admiral Bull Halsey, of World War II fame in the battles of the Pacific, said his worst assignment of the war was when he commanded an LSD—Large Steel Desk! But any student of history who knows Admiral Halsey also knows he didn't win the war in the Pacific sitting behind that LSD.

And you'll get things done only when you get out where things are happening and where you can see how your orders are being carried out.

It's three o'clock in the morning.

"Some plant managers who have a three shift operation 24 hours around the clock never set their foot in the door after five in the afternoon," says Sam Wheeler, president of Wheeler Management Consultants. "But that suits me just fine. His failure to do a job makes a living for me!

"When we're called in to find the bottlenecks in a plant, 95 percent of the time I find the problem exists because that plant manager didn't get out of his plush wigaboo to find out what's going on outside his own door—*especially on the third shift at three o'clock in the morning!*

"I can tell amost every time where the problem is when we first go into the plant," Sam says. "If the manager has reams of paper, correspondence, and all kinds of reports on his desk plus a whole staff of assistants all there waiting to answer our questions—for he can't—I know immediately that he's our bottleneck. He doesn't know his own operation because he's never really seen it!"

Learn a man's name.

If you want an employee to like you and respect you, you must remember who he is. He'll remember who you are. I know there are a lot more of him to remember than there is of you, but he'll never stop to think of that. So remember his name, and preferably his first one. Whenever you do, you pay him a compliment of the highest order. And it doesn't matter whether you employ ten men, a hundred or a thousand, he'll expect you to know. And he's right—you should.

"I absolutely refuse to answer to *Hey—you!*" says Frank Ward, the letter carrier who delivers mail to my house. "I don't mind being Mr. Postman, Mr. Mailman, or Uncle Sam, but *Hey-You!* is pushing it too far. I just won't answer. I have close to 500 stops on my route and I know every name in each family. I don't necessarily expect them to know mine, but I do expect them to know what and who I am!"

8. Have the courage to make a decision — take a risk — accept the responsibility.

Lastly, I would say that even if you stumble and fall, even if you fail to follow the previous seven guidelines properly at all times, your people will give you credit for trying and they'll stick with you if you have the fortitude to do your best on this one—number eight.

No one likes a coward—either physical or mental. The brilliant thinker who has not the courage to take the first forward step that he himself advocates is despised by his colleagues. He accomplishes nothing unless he possesses the courage to act upon his own convictions.

Brigham Young, the leader of the Mormon trek to Utah, succeeded, not only because he thought of a plan to take his followers to a place of safety hundreds of miles away from religious persecution, but also because he had the courage to act and to put his own plan into effect in spite of all the hardships and all the difficulties he knew they would face on the way. He also had the courage to accept the full responsibility in case of failure.

And so did Washington and Lincoln, Roosevelt and Truman, Eisenhower and MacArthur, and a thousand more who had the same capacity for leadership.

The last word.

To have your subordinates like you and respect you, you must practice the law of reversal that you learned back in Chapter One. You must like and respect them first. When you do, you're well on your way to becoming a good boss. Knowledge of your people will help you, but it'll take more than that. It will take wisdom and a deep appreciation and understanding of them and their individual problems.

And it will also require that you follow these eight guidelines:

1. *Always set the example.*
2. *Don't set up your own standards of right and wrong.*
3. *Don't expect them to agree with everything you say or do.*
4. *Make allowances for their inexperience.*

5. *Always be considerate.*

6. *Give ground on trifles—never on principles.*

7. *You must see—and be seen!*

8. *You must have the courage to make a decision—take a risk—accept your responsibility.*

When you practice these guidelines, I can assure you that you'll be a better boss and that your employees will like you and respect you. But whether they really love you or not is entirely up to you.

You Can't Win Them All!

For fourteen chapters now I've been telling you how you can benefit and how you can profit when you know the secrets of controlling people—the real know-how of supervision. But I'd be entirely remiss if I didn't tell you that *you can't win them all!* There are always going to be some who just won't respond, no matter how much you try to help them.

However, not all of that small group of problem employees are going to fall by the wayside, either. You'll still be able to save some of them. And it's to your benefit to salvage as many of them as you can. Why? Because it's so costly to recruit and train a new employee. That's why!

Unskilled labor might be easy to come by, true enough. But the skilled employee, the highly competent technician, the able administrator, the capable executive, didn't become well-trained overnight. They're all expensive to train and they're hard to replace, so *it's to your advantage and your benefit to turn as many of them as you can into good, dependable, loyal, and productive employees.*

Even the last private in the rear rank is valuable.

"When I was in Fort Riley, Kansas, commanding a basic training company, a certain private—a basic trainee whom I well remember—was transferred to me," says Charlie Lawrence, now in an executive position with Burroughs.

"He'd been in the army twenty weeks, but had yet to finish his eight weeks of basic training. He'd been AWOL and in the stockade. Three previous company commanders had given up on him.

"When he reported to me, I made both his position and mine very clear. 'What you've done before—I don't care!' I told him. 'All that counts is what you do now for me. You can either soldier or not soldier, it's up to you. If you do, I'll back you all the way, and *your past will be wiped out*. If you don't—I'll throw you to the wolves! It's all up to you.'

"He ended up as one of my honor graduates. He wasn't bad at all. He'd just gotten off on the wrong foot and everybody expected him to stay that way. I didn't. I started him off with a clean slate, without any prejudice whatever. He came through for me, and much more important—for himself. He became a valuable soldier to the army."

Protect your investment.

Saving a man as Charlie Lawrence did is not only the decent thing to do, it also protects your investment. For example, Zenith trains its employees for sixteen weeks at company expense. Woolworth conducts a retail training program for their junior executives. In both cases, there's a big *IF:* If the man agrees to stay with the company for a specified time. If a man wants to attend one of the military service's advanced schools, he must sign a commitment to remain on duty for a definite number of additional years. All these companies and organizations are simply protecting their original investments.

What are you going to do, for example, about the ball of fire who ends up an alcoholic at 40? Or the man who decided to retire *on his job* at 35 feeling that the company still owes him a living? Or the chronic absentee? Or the neurotic? Are you going to fire them all? I doubt it. That's not an answer, except in the case of the completely incorrigible employee. The rest of them, at least, in most cases, can be salvaged and made into good, dependable employees again.

You have to do something positive if you want to protect your investment. If you don't, you'll end up like the army replacing a good man every two years. Few companies can afford to do that. The small group that causes you trouble can be divided again into three smaller subgroups.

1. The completely incorrigible employee.

Because of people like these, we still maintain jails and reformatories and penitentiaries. Most of these people seem to be constitutionally incapable of being honest with themselves. They cannot learn to work with others, obey orders, accept discipline from a higher authority, or discipline themselves.

Perhaps they are not at fault; I do not know. I am not a psychologist nor a psychiatrist, and a deep study of these people is their problem—not ours. Such a study is far beyond the scope of this book on supervision. From a managerial or a supervisory point of view, the important thing is to identify the incorrigible employee, and eliminate him as quickly as possible.

You see, many of these incorrigibles seem to have been born that way. They are by their very nature not able to grasp and develop a manner of living that demands rigorous and upright honesty. Unfortunately, this small percentage of humanity seems destined for the gutter or the prison and nothing on earth that you or I can do will seem to stop him.

The answer, then? There is none, at least as far as you're concerned. You're a businessman—not a social worker. *You can't win them all, and he's one of the ones you can't win!* And since you're not running a rehabilitation center or a philanthropy, you have no choice in this matter. If he's a member of your management team—*fire him!* If he's a member of organized labor, you'll have to do the same thing; it'll just take a little longer, that's all.

2. The critic.

Now that you've fired the incorrigible employee, I want you to take a look at that nuisance, *the critic,* also known as *the sharpshooter, the know-it-all.* Every plant always has their fair share of him and a little extra to spare. According to his way of thinking, no one in a management position ever does anything right, that is, if you'll listen to his measured opinion. He delights in causing embarrassment to a supervisor, a foreman, or anyone else in a position of authority.

This individual is easily recognized. His ideas on how to improve—how to run the show—will almost always be given to you in public in a loud voice so that all within range can hear. *And his suggestions will always be given in a manner that's calculated to embarass you.*

The sharpshooter derives his pleasure primarily from the idea that you don't know what's actually going on in your own shop. He hopes to expose your ignorance and make a fool of you. If you know your job, you have no problem at all. And since you know what his goal is, it's usually just as easy to dispose of him as it is to identify him. If you know the enemy's intentions, you really are foolish if you don't take the proper countermeasures.

Don't let him get to you; that's what he's trying to do. You'll need only to use patience, common sense, and above all, you'll need to keep a tight rein on your temper.

You can handle this situation successfully by doing exactly what Casey Stengel always wanted to do. Simply invite him to put down his hot dog and come down out of the stands and show you how to do it! Listen to how Barry Sloan, a foreman with Briggs & Stratton, does it:

"I get all surrounding activity stopped so everyone can hear—and believe me, that's easy enough to do," says Barry. "Everyone wants to hear. Then I say, 'your idea sounds excellent, Tom. And it sounds as if you'd spent a lot of time figuring out how to do it. Tell you what. I wish you'd do me a favor right now and show the rest of us exactly how you propose to do it. I'd like to see a little demonstration of your idea for I value your opinion a great deal!' "

Very good method. This will catch your sharpshooter completely off-guard. He expects you to charge out of your corner swinging at the first sound of the bell. He can now do only one of two things. He has no other choice. He can show you that he does have a good idea and that it's worthwhile, or he'll clam up and retreat in haste and confusion amid the laughter of his fellow employees. His nature is such that he can't tolerate too many defeats like that; you may make a good employee out of him almost by default.

The only time this man really becomes a problem is when you let him bug you. Don't let him get to you, then. That's all he wants; that's why he's playing his silly game.

3. The real problem case.

There's only one standard to use to determine whether a person belongs in this category or not. It's very simple to decide. *He has to be hurting either your production or your profit!* How can you determine this? Easy.

All you have to do is ask yourself three simple questions about this man. If you can't answer *yes* to one of them, sorry to disillusion you, but that man's not really a problem after all—*no matter how much you personally dislike him!*

a. Does he underperform in his job?

Is his work below the accepted norm in both quality and quantity? Does he produce fewer units than he should in an average work day? Does he have excessive waste or a high turn-back rate from your quality control section? In other words, *does he in some tangible and visible way fail to measure up to the reasonable performance standards you've set for him?* If your answer is *yes* to any of these basic questions—*you have a problem case on your hands.*

b. Does he interfere with the work of others?

Do you always find him at the bottom of employee disturbances? Does his inferior quality of work prevent another department from functioning? Does his failure to produce the proper amount cause another worker or another section to shut down temporarily? If so—*you have a problem.*

c. Does he cause harm to his own group?

If he's part of a team or a group, do other members of that work unit try to leave his group? Do people refuse to transfer to his work group? Is he causing some of his own team members a financial loss? If you have to answer *yes* to any of these questions, *you have a problem case to solve.*

Judge him by this standard.

I'm sure you can see that if he underperforms in his job, if he interferes with the work of others, or if he causes harm to his own work group, then *he's causing a problem by hurting your production and cutting into your profit.*

And that makes him your problem to solve. He's the last one to take care of. You got rid of the incorrigible; you disposed of the sharpshooter. Now how to handle this man is your question. First of all, who is he? What's he like?

Well, he could fit any one of a number of types. He could be a hand-sitter, a do-nothing, a boat-misser, a promotion pass-over, a loner, an empire builder, even a good guy, maybe even a genius.

No matter what or who he is, if he's causing you trouble in any one of these three basic areas—if you answer *yes* to any of those questions about his performance, then he's a problem to you. Let me show you just a couple of examples so you can get the feel of what I mean. We don't have time to discuss all of them.

Even a genius can be a problem.

Maybe he really is a brilliant man. Maybe he gives you everything you want—does everything you ask him to do. But if he *thinks* he's a genius, chances are he'll be a nonconformist. Might even work better at night than in the day. So you'll have to learn to live with him and satisfy his peculiar needs, *that is, if you're willing to go along with him* since he gives you everything you want. However—

"I can't agree with that idea at all," says Jack Gray, a member of the board of IBM. "Nobody's that valuable! I've got a cousin who retired out of the air force as a general. Didn't think they could get along without him! Only person who remembers him is the finance officer who sends him a retirement check every month—*and he's one of our own IBM machines!*

"You see, there's a certain office discipline even a genius has to live with," Mr. Gray says. "Even if he does everything you want— even if he does more—when he doesn't show up for work or he's late, people wonder. They get suspicious—even jealous. 'Is he really that valuable?' they ask. I don't think so. I think he can be a destructive force! He hurts morale so much you have to answer *yes* to two of those three questions about performance and profit. *He's definitely interfering with the work of others and he's causing harm to his own group.* Custer and Napoleon were geniuses, according to some; look at what happened to them!

"So I repeat. No one's that valuable. No one's indispensable. If that were true, we couldn't afford to let a true genius die, and no one gets out of life alive!"

Or what about the loner?

A loner is a potential alcoholic, first of all. Even if he doesn't eventually qualify for the funny farm, he causes problems simply because he can't communicate with people. The world's getting too small and too crowded for hermits any more.

"In my experience, I've found you can never really change a loner," says Bob Masters, sales manager for Heathkit. "Even in a business like ours which is 95 percent mail order, we can't use a man who's an introvert. Truthfully, I'd a lot rather hire a weaker man who's organization minded! I want no part of the loner. I think he's got some sort of a personality defect."

Your biggest problem of all: the alcoholic!

The alcoholic employee is your greatest problem—be he (or she) executive, salesman, skilled workman, technician, or secretary. When he's sober, he's usually dependable and normally quite intelligent, often even brilliant, but when he's drunk or suffering from a severe hangover, he's like a berserk animal.

Since he is going to be your biggest problem child, I'd like to devote more time and space to him than to some of the lesser problem types. Let me first give you some facts and figures I got from the National Council on Alcoholism, 2 East 103rd Street, New York, 10029, so we'll be on some common ground here. Incidentally, they have an Industrial Services Division which will be glad to help you solve the drinking problems of any of your company employees who suffer from alcoholism.

Roughly, at the present time, somewhere between six and a half to seven million people in the United States suffer from alcoholism. As the population increases, so will the number of alcoholics, but for statistical purposes, let me tell you that *one out of every thirteen people who drinks becomes an alcoholic.*

So what!

"So what!" you say. "What's that to me? I'm not an alcoholic and I'll not hire one. I don't go down to skid row to hire my employees!"

I have news for you, my friend. Only three percent of the alcoholics ever make it down to skid row. Ninety-seven percent of all alcoholics are individuals with jobs and homes—fathers and mothers—husbands and wives—teachers, lawyers, doctors, ministers, farmers, salesmen, businessmen—industrial executives and production workers—your next door neighbors.

Each alcoholic affects the lives—often tragically—of at least four other persons. According to life insurance statistics, the life span of an alcoholic is twelve years shorter than the national average.

Alcoholism is involved in more than fifty percent of the automobile accident deaths that occur each year. Alcoholism does incalculable damage to personal and family life—it is a leading cause of separation, divorce, desertion, and *emotional problems which carry over into the individual's business or work.*

Getting more interested now? Then listen to the next bit of information; it'll really hit you where it hurts—right in the pocketbook!

The cost of alcoholism to American business and industry in absenteeism, fringe benefits, loss of trained manpower, inefficiency, and accidents *far exceeds two billion dollars a year!*

More than 2,500,000 workers—an estimated three to five percent of the work force—suffer from alcoholism. Ninety percent of the alcoholics in any company remain hidden until they become completely unemployable.

The alcoholic employee averages two to three times as much absenteeism and has twice as many accidents on the job as the nonalcoholic.

Dr. John MacIver, the Director of United States Steel's Psychiatric Services, says, *"Alcoholism is the largest behavioral problem in industry!"*

How alcoholism can cost you money.

Here's what can happen to you and to your business specifically. One of your technicians with a shaky hand and a heavy hangover turns the wrong valve; he spoils a batch of chemicals worth three to four times his annual salary.

Your secretary, edgy and jumpy from a night on the town, incorrectly addresses an envelope and your company bid fails to make the deadline when the postman returns it—*Addressee Unknown.*

Your sales director, who's been a trusted executive of your company for years, goes on a sudden drinking spree. He fails to show up at a crucial meeting and loses your biggest account for you. Impossible! you say? Happens every day!

Alcoholism causes most of the military's problems.

Henry Richmond, formerly the Deputy Provost Marshal of the Fifth Army, and now a practicing attorney in Washington, D.C., told me that almost all of the problems in the service came from alcoholism.

"I'd not be afraid to say that ninety-nine and nine-tenths percent of the problems in the military come from the alcoholic soldier," Henry says, "All you have to do is look at the military police desk blotter in any post. Car accidents? Driving under the influence. Domestic disturbances? Drunken husband beating up on the wife or the kids. Petty thievery by the children in the post exchange or the commissary? No money at home; everything's spent on booze. If it weren't for liquor and alcoholism, most military police would be out of a job."

What some companies are doing about their problem.

If I were to list all the companies and corporations that have some sort of an alcoholism program, it might look like the New York Stock Exchange. So I'll just give credit to some of the pioneers in the field.

You'll encounter such familiar names as United States Steel, American Telephone and Telegraph, International Business Machines, Republic Steel, Eastman Kodak, Du Pont, Allis-Chalmers, Kaiser Industries. . . .

Many industries today sponsor Alcoholics Anonymous groups right in their plants as well as getting qualified professional assistance from the National Council on Alcoholism. By using modern administrative and management techniques in setting up formal employee alcoholism information programs, the Industrial Services Division has demonstrated that it is possible to achieve a recovery rate of from fifty to seventy percent among those company employees who are alcoholic.

With this recovery rate come measurable results for the company, too. These benefits come in the form of increased efficiency, conservation of valuable manpower, reduced absenteeism, lowered production costs, increased quality of workmanship, and better relationships between and among management and production employees.

These are important factors to consider in these days of increasing competition. Forward looking managers are always interested in any type of a program which can show concrete results in increasing efficiency, reducing waste, conserving manpower, and cutting costs. I would be; wouldn't you?

This chapter wasn't meant to be a lecture on alcoholism alone. But I did feel that it was important enough to give a rather extensive coverage to it since it is your biggest employee problem, whether you realize it yet or not. So I make no apology for the extra pages devoted to this important health problem. And yet—I've barely scratched the surface.

If you do want more information, contact the National Council on Alcoholism, or drop a line to the General Service Headquarters for Alcoholics Anonymous, Post Office Box 459, Grand Central Station, New York, 10017. Both of these organizations can give you much more information on how to handle the alcoholic problem in your plant. I can only call it to your attention; from this distance I can't solve it for you.

The key to all behavioral problems is discipline.

Now I'm going to go out on a limb and say that the answer to all your problems is discipline. (Even the reformed alcoholic will tell you that he got sober through self-discipline.) The key to all effective discipline lies in one word—*training*.

"The officer who trains his men by discipline must use the whip, for to him discipline is punishment," says Colonel Emmet Hogan. "But the officer who disciplines by training seldom requires it. To him, discipline is achieved, not by the lash and punishment but by training, and he's right. Good training overcomes resistance to obedience and resentment of authority. When obedience becomes habitual, natural, and willing, *training has paid off in terms of properly disciplined soldiers.*"

And what about industry?

The same concept holds true. Discipline by training; don't train by discipline. This will help you achieve your true goal of self-discipline. The man who works only when the boss is around is not self-disciplined. And you can't always be around. You must trust your employees, but you can trust them only when they discipline themselves.

Of course, all men are different. The degree to which you can trust each individual employee to discipline himself and the amount of supervisory attention you must give him will vary with each one. Some employees will show by their attitudes and their behavior that they are capable of self-discipline from the first day they start to work for you. Others may need a little more help—a push in the right direction. You can start them on the right path when they first go to work for you by using—

An orientation program.

Your orientation program should be used to acquaint each new employee with the general policies and the general regulations under which he's going to work. It should never be used as a whip to *get him in line the first thing!* If you have a good orientation program to give him a start in the right direction, he'll soon learn the *mold* or the *pattern* he's expected to fit into.

On-the-job training is involved with discipline.

Training a man on his new job teaches him discipline. You are responsible for teaching this new employee, either in class or on the job, so he will know the skills and the procedures he'll need to perform his duties. You might not think initially that on-the-job training is discipline, but it is a vital part of your whole program to develop that man's self-discipline. Remember what Colonel Hogan said? *Training pays off in terms of disciplined workers.* When your employee can do his job without you standing over him, he is most definitely a self-disciplined worker.

The safety inspector can help you.

A factory is no longer a safe place to work unless you take the necessary precautions. Tiny men control giant machines. Ever see a calendar in a rubber plant? A careless operator can lose an arm in less than two seconds! Can you imagine what could happen if a man gets careless in an oil refinery with cigarettes? Or street shoes in a steel foundry?

A careless employee lacks discipline; he has not been properly trained. That's why your safety inspector is so important. By showing new employees the safety hazards in your plant, he can teach them the importance of self-discipline.

The immediate supervisor is the key man.

Most of the training program—and therefore, the discipline—falls on the shoulders of the employee's immediate supervisor. He approves the employment of new men and he gives them a certain amount of orientation in his own department. The front-line supervisor is responsible for their on-the-job training. Often the breaking of rules and regulations comes from poor training and improper communication. All this is a part of discipline.

Job-performance evaluation is also a part of your program.

Through this management technique, you can appraise the workman's job performance—both as to quantity and quality—his attitude toward his job and his general overall behavior. This is a very definite method which you can use to mold a man to the pattern that you want.

However, self-discipline should be your final goal for your employee. The true leader wants to get the man *on his own* as soon as humanly possible. Only the martinet enjoys using the whiplash of punishment.

Final Check Points.

You might not be able to win them all when you finish this chapter, but you'll come mighty close to it. You'll be able to influence and control and properly motivate about 97 to 98 percent of the people who work for you, and that's an excellent percentage.

You shouldn't lose anyone permanently except the incorrigible employee. Oh, you'll lose a few now and then temporarily, but they'll always be back in there stronger than ever in a day or so. You don't have to win every campaign to achieve the final victory. So stay right in there and keep punching!

P.S.
If It Ain't Broke — Why Fix It?

If your men are griping a little, don't worry about it. Worry about them when they're not! A man's not feeling well unless he can beef about something. Even if you were a perfect boss, they'd complain because they had nothing to complain about! So let them blow off steam; do 'em good. Works like a safety valve. Here's how to know whether it's healthy griping or not:

If everything's running smooth as silk, if production is soaring and profits are jumping, it's just good healthy griping. When the fish are biting, don't change the bait. Just go take a nap, my friend. Don't make any waves. Don't meddle. Don't be a worry wart or a fuss budget. Easy does it.

If you had an alarm clock that was still running well and had gotten you up every morning on time for the last twenty years, would you suddenly decide to take it apart and check just to see if it would ring for sure tomorrow morning? I wouldn't either.

So if it ain't broke—don't fix it!